The Untold Story of
Izola Ware Curry

When Harlem Saved A King

A.L. Cohen

DEDICATION

I dedicate this book to the millions of people around the world that are suffering with Mental Illness. If you are seeking help, I praise you for your bravery and desire to better your mental state of mind. If you have not yet sought help for whatever reason, I pray that you will find the strength and courage to seek help.

If a person you care about is in crisis, please encourage them to seek help immediately. Direct them to call 1-900-273-TALK (8225). To reach a   24-hour crisis center, text MHA to 741741, call 911, or go to the nearest emergency room. You can also call these numbers if you fear for someone's safety or life. Call 911 or go to the nearest emergency room if you are in need of immediate help.

CONTENTS

National Council of Negro Women
Mary McLeod Bethune
founded 1935

Dorothy Height

Minton's
Christmas (New
Ball Years
Q Jr.)

ACKNOWLEDGMENTS

This book would not have been possible without the support
and dedication of my wife Janet, who has spent countless hours
and days in assuring that the information and the research in
this book is accurate. I want to thank her also for continuing to
be a wife, a mother and a business partner all at the same time.
She is truly my best friend and a gift from God.

To La-Tressa Lane, thank you for your hard work and
dedication working alongside my wife.

Violet Mae Watson
(1891 — 1971)
wife of James S.
Watson, first black judge
in NY state
mother of US customs
Court Judge James
L Watson
Founder National Council
of Negro
Women

jack and jill clubs
black upper class

1 INTRODUCTION

I was brought in by Touro College of Osteopathic Medicine in 2011 as the Director of Community Affairs. As a Jewish medical school in the middle of Harlem, Touro College had no idea how to be inclusive in the community of which they were located. It was clear there was much work to be done and I needed to get right to it!

During my initial days at Touro I began to do research on the history of the college. My goal was to discover ways to integrate minorities into the college and bring Touro a level of awareness that could allow them to become a contributor in the community. I knew if I were to find out more about the history of Touro and the decision to open in Harlem I could build upon that in the development of community initiatives.

In my research, I was shocked and appalled to learn that what was now Touro College of Osteopathic Medicine was once a Jewish owned department store, Blumstein's. Even more astonishing to me, I found a few articles that described a stabbing, an attempted assassination, on the late Dr. Martin Luther King Jr. What! Dr. King had been stabbed? How did I not know about this? I grew up hearing, reading, and watching featured films about the life of one of the greatest civil rights leaders in our history. Every facet of his personal, professional and spiritual life had been probed and put under a microscope for public view and consumption. How did we not know that he was stabbed in Harlem in 1958?

I was so surprised that I began to ask other people such as politicians and even historians all of whom had the same reaction as I did. Most replied, "No way! We would have known about this." When a few historians told me that they had heard an account of a story similar to what was reflected in the articles, I knew it was a piece of unknown history that must be shared and I was going to take some responsibility in shedding a light of awareness on this untold story.

I had a daunting task ahead of me. What really happened on September 20, 1958 in Blumstein's Department Store? What really happened in Harlem Hospital? What happened to Izola Ware Curry? Did Curry act alone? While we will recount facts about the late Dr. Martin Luther King Jr., we will spend most of our time heavily indulging in the little known details that occurred at Blumstein's Department Store in Harlem, New York on September 20, 1958.

This book will explore the events surrounding the stabbing and whether or not this woman from Adrian, Georgia acted alone. The Izola Ware Curry biopic gives readers a glimpse into the mind of one of America's lesser known would-be assassins. Unlike the more infamous political assassins such as Jack Ruby, Lee Harvey Oswald and Sirhan Sirhan, Curry is a long forgotten figure in American history. Who is Izola Ware Curry? What was her fascination with Dr. King? Was she apart of a larger plot by the White Citizens Council, the white supremacy group responsible for the death of Medgar Evers in 1963? We will explore the life, mental illness allegations and motivations of Izola Ware Curry.

When I was bols

Figure 1: Blumstein's Department Store in Harlem, NY March 21, 1954
Wurts. Bros *from the collection of the Museum of the City of New*
York http://collections.mcny.org/C.aspx?VP3=SearchResult_VPage&VBID=24UAYW
W4
GPO&SMLS=1&RW=1366&RH=631

Figure 2: Blumstein's Department Store in Harlem, NY 1957 credit, Flickr

Figure 3: Touro College of Osteopathic Medicine in Harlem, NY

Figure 4: Launch of Touro College in 2007, The Sun Reporter
- Credit Konrad Fiedler

2 HISTORY

America in 1958

The year 1958 in America was a crossroad in history stuck between the past and the present. It's 1958 and America is beginning to change more rapidly than ever before in its existence. Stuck at a crossroad in history between the past and present, innovations both technological and cultural sweep across the nation.

As a response to the Russian's Sputnik, America successfully launches Explorer 1 into orbit, becoming the first ever American satellite in space. A few months later President Eisenhower will establish NASA, officially starting the decades long "The Space Race".

Elvis Presley is inducted in the U.S. Army. A 14-year old prodigy named Bobby Fischer wins the US Chess Championship. The Hula Hoop craze sweeps across the nation.

1958 bought Americans a recession with a vengeance and large increases in unemployment at over 7.0% (5.2 million). In that same year inflation dipped below 2% so those employed that averaged wages of $3,851 per year were quite well off. Cars continued to get bigger and heavier with larger engines, but imports continued to grow now with the added Datsun and more Toyotas from Japan.

America's first satellite was launched from Cape Canaveral. This is also the year that the microchip was first developed, which is the very early stages of the personal computer (PC) being used at work and in homes today.

On June 30, 1958 Congress passed a law authorizing the admission of Alaska as the 49th state in the Union, the first new state since 1912. The senate passed the Alaska statehood bill by a vote of 64-20.

In July 1958, Mildred Loving (1940-2008), a woman of American Indian and black heritage, and her white husband, Richard (d.1975), were arrested in Virginia within weeks of arriving from Washington, DC and convicted on charges of cohabiting as man and wife. In 1967 the supreme court in Loving v. Virginia, struck down state laws prohibiting interracial marriages.

On September 2, 1958 President Eisenhower signed the National Defense Education Act, which provided aid to public and private education to promote learning in such fields as math and science. Later that month on September 12, 1958, The US Supreme Court, in Cooper v. Aaron, unanimously ruled that Arkansas officials who were resisting public school desegregation orders could not disregard the high court's rulings.

On September 22, 1958 Sherman Adams, assistant to President Eisenhower, resigned amid charges of improperly using his influence to help an industrialist. Critics of the

Eisenhower Administration called Chief Presidential Advisor Sherman Adams the "Assistant President" because they considered him to be too powerful. Adams was the former

governor of New Hampshire. He resigned after it was revealed that a Boston industrialist had given him gifts in exchange for preferential treatment before the Federal Trade Commission(FTC) and Securities Exchange Commission (SEC).

It's December 28, 1958 at Yankee Stadium, the Baltimore Colts (23) beat the NY Giants(17) in the first NFL Championship game to ever go into overtime.

Yes, change was everywhere, and at the very forefront is Harlem, New York.

Figure 5: Explorer 1 was officially launched into orbit, 1958 – Credited Space.com

Figure 6: Elvis Presley was sworn into the U.S. Army – Credited Reddit

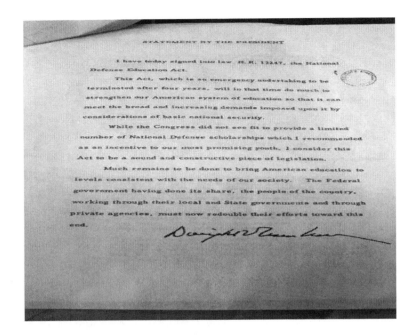

Figure 7:: National Defense Act of 1958 was signed by President Eisenhower

Harlem in 1958

In 1958, Harlem was in a celebratory mood. In March, Sugar Ray Robinson regained his middleweight title beating Carmen Basilio in fifteen rounds. Hometown hero Althea Gibson became the first African American woman voted Woman Athlete of the Year. Later that summer she would go on to win the Olympic Gold medal in both the singles and doubles match.

This was also the year that Harlem native James Baldwin returned to the U.S. from France with a freshly minted copy of his new novel, Giovanni's Room. His friend and sometimes adversary, Malcolm X, was appointed to head of the Nation of Islam's Mosque #7 in Harlem.

On March 30, Alvin Ailey and a group of young, black modern dancers perform for the first time as members of Alvin Ailey American Dance Theater.

Photographer Art Kane assembled 51 jazz musicians on 127th street for his portrait entitled, *A Great day in Harlem*. Yes, it was a great day in Harlem and, in fact, it had every appearance of being a great year in Harlem until the fall.

In the 1950s the Civil Rights Movement in America began to gain mainstream attention for the first time. While segregation was still prevalent throughout the nation, African Americans of all ages began to protest Jim Crow laws in ways that the white public could no longer ignore.

In 1955, Rosa Parks refused to give up her seat on a segregated bus. That same year Emmett Till was murdered for whistling at a white woman, inspiring one of the first national debates about the Jim Crow laws in the South. Two years later in 1957, one of the first major sit-ins took place at the Royal Ice Cream Parlor in Durham, North Carolina. An event organized by Reverend Douglas E. Moore, a former classmate of Dr. Martin Luther King Jr. at Boston University.

Harlem didn't have the same kind of segregation problems that cities in the South had, but nonetheless, it was a major hub of activity for the Civil Rights Movement. At the forefront was Harlem's de factor leader, Malcom X. While his rise to power was viewed as a beacon of hope to the Harlem community, his philosophies often times conflicted with the pacifist demonstrations being led by Reverend Moore and Reverend King.

While Malcolm X was Harlem's leader on the ground, Adam Clayton Powell Jr. was its voice in Washington. The first person from New York of African-American descent to be elected to Congress. Congressman Powell would go on to represent Harlem in the House of Representatives for over 25 years, becoming one of the most powerful black men in all of Washington, DC. However, his career wasn't devoid of controversy, including one with someone who would go on to become one of Dr. Martin Luther King Jr.'s closest confidants, a gay Quaker, named Bayard Rustin.

Bayard Rustin was an eccentric for his time. After moving to Harlem in 1936 to become a nightclub singer, Mr. Rustin quickly became an activist for Civil Rights. A master strategist and tireless activist, Bayard Rustin is best remembered as the organizer of the 1963 March on Washington, one of the largest nonviolent protests ever held in the United States. He was one of the main organizers of The Journey of Reconciliation, a 1947 non-violent protest of the segregation laws in the South, an act that would go on to inspire Freedom Rides of the 1960's. Freedom Riders were civil rights activist who rode interstate buses into the segregated United States. Rustin was a Pacifist with Communist affiliations. Those who identified themselves as pacifist were strongly against "war" and violence as a mean to peace. On the contrary, those who identified themselves as communist believed that social and economic war (classism) was justifiable. Rustin was arrested in 1953 for sexual activity with two other men in a parked car, a crime that he would serve 60 days in jail for.

It wasn't until 1956 that Bayard Rustin met Dr. Martin Luther King Jr.. After hearing about King's ongoing Montgomery Bus Boycott, Bayard left his post as executive secretary of the War Resisters League, and went down to Montgomery, Alabama to offer his services. The War Resisters League was founded in 1923 by men and women who had opposed World War I, in which many of its founders had been jailed for refusing military service. He immediately convinced Dr. King to abandon his guns and embrace Gandhian protest techniques to the American Civil Rights Movement, and helped mold Dr. King into an international symbol of peace and nonviolence which he had not personally embraced initially. In fact, there were guns inside King's house, and armed guards posted at his doors prior to meeting Rustin.

Rustin also brilliantly suggested that King and the rest of the protesters turn themselves in at the local jail instead of waiting for the police to arrest them like common criminals. This shrewd tactic would go on to be the turning point of the entire boycott, eventually leading the Supreme Court to outlaw segregation on all Montgomery buses. Despite these achievements, Rustin was silenced, threatened, arrested, beaten, imprisoned and fired from important leadership positions, largely because he was an openly gay man.

Rustin would go on to become one of Dr. King's most trusted advisors as well as the main organizer of his 1963 March on Washington. However, perhaps his most significant contribution was introducing Dr. Martin Luther King Jr. to a wealthy Jewish Communist named Stanley Levison.

Figure 8: Great Day In Harlem Portrait

Figure 9: Adam Clayton Powell in the streets of Harlem NY 1958

Figure 11: Rustin and King together - Credited advocate.com

Figure 10: Rustin and King together in 1957

3 STRIDE TOWARD FREEDOM

When Stanley David Levison died in 1979, Coretta Scott King called him, "Truly one of the great unsung heroes in the nonviolent struggle for justice and social decency in the twentieth-century America... Few people know of the magnitude of his contributions to the labor, Civil Rights, and peace movements." Indeed Levison was one of the most influential figures in not just Dr. King's life, but in the entire Civil Rights Movement. He was also perhaps the most unique: a white, independently wealthy, non-practicing Jew with deep communist ties. Levison eventually became King's most trusted friend and advisor, a relationship that would stay strong until King's untimely death.

A native New Yorker, Levison earned his law degree from St. John's University in 1939. Upon graduating, instead of practicing law, he invested in laundromats and car dealerships. This led to him becoming extremely wealthy before the age of thirty-five.

Influenced living through the Depression, Levison became a radical activist for human rights, aligning himself with the civil rights advocacy of the Communist Party and fighting hard against the McCarthyism of the 1950's. It was through these labor movement channels that Levison met Bayard Rustin, and soon the two of them, along with former NAACP official Ella Jo Baker, formed In Friendship, an organization established to help raise funds for combatting racial discrimination.

Watsons ?,

It was on January 5, 1956, after the Montgomery bus boycott that In Friendship was formed with a primary common goal to direct economic aid to the South's growing civil rights struggle. Ella Jo Baker, Stanley Levison, Bayard Rustin and representatives from more than 25 religious, political, and labor groups sought to assist grassroots activists who were "suffering economic reprisals because of their fight against segregation" through In Friendship. During its three years of operation, the organization contributed thousands of dollars to support the work of Dr. Martin Luther King Jr. and the Montgomery Improvement Association (MIA). King stated in a letter to a chairman of In Friendship, George Lawrence "We are very grateful to 'In Friendship' for the interest that it has taken in our struggle" (Papers 3:408)

In May of 1956, In Friendship joined with the Brotherhood of sleeping Car Porters to hold a civil rights rally in New York City's Madison Square Garden. The funds received during this rally went to MIA and National Association for the Advancement of Colored People (NAACP) with an additional $10,000 being deposited into the Victory Savings Bank in Columbia, South Carolina, to enable the bank to issue loans to need in Columbia, South Carolina, to enable the bank to issue loans to needy tenant farmers.

In Friendship held its second major fundraiser on December 5, 1956. It was a concert at New York's Manhattan Center to commemorate the first anniversary of the start of the bus boycott. In a November 23 letter to concert organizers Ruth Bunche and Aminda Wilkins, King described how boycotters were forced to walk to work because of a recent legal ban on carpools and how drivers were being targeted for economic retaliation. King wrote, "These factors mean that we are unfortunately in grave need of funds for carrying on the most critical phase of our struggle" (Papers 3:437). The event raised nearly $2,000 for the MIA. Coretta King spoke at the fundraiser telling the crowd the story of the old woman who said, "It used to be my soul was tired while my feet rested. Now my feet are tired but my soul is resting" (King, 5 December 1956)

In Friendship continued to aid the movement after the bus boycott came to an end. In 1957 funds were raised to assist in the preparations for the January 1957 Southern Negro Leaders Conference, The founding gathering of the Southern Christian Leadership Conference. The organization later contributed $500 toward King's 1957 trip to Ghana and secured $4,000 grant for his 1959 India trip. During the late 1950s, In friendship disbanded after funds dwindled as donors began directing their contributions directly to movement groups and Baker, Levison, and Rustin became involved with the SCLC.

The In Friendship organization led to Levison meeting Dr. Martin Luther King Jr. in 1956 during the Montgomery Bus Boycotts. After seeing the power of the southern civil rights movement in person, Levison and Rustin suggested establishing a new organization that could capitalize on the up swell of National support that the Montgomery Bus Boycott had engendered. Thus the South Christian Leadership Conference was created, and by a Jew nonetheless.

By 1958, King and Levison had become incredibly close, talking on the phone almost daily. King would offer Levison payment for the work he did with the SCLC but Levison always refused stating: "The liberation struggle is the most positive and rewarding area of work anyone could experience."

It was Levison who suggested that King write a book about his experiences with the bus boycott. He soon secured a publishing deal with Harper Bro. for Dr. Martin Luther King Jr.'s first book, *Stride Toward Freedom.*

Levison supervised the project from start to finish. He

heavily   *he*

fiercely edited King's writing, and along with Bayard Rustin, wrote his own passages that would end up in the published text, however both him and Rustin refused to take credit out of fear that their status as "communist agitators" would distract from the books message.

Nine months after beginning the project, the manuscript was finished, and *Stride Toward Freedom* was scheduled for publication on September 17, 1958. The question remained, how best to launch the book to the masses. Levison had the perfect plan. Bring Dr. King to Harlem, New York for a public coronation of the Civil Rights Movement's newest leader. The book signing was scheduled to take place at Blumstein's Department store

Figure 12: Dr. King's first book, Stride Toward Freedom

on September 20, 1958, however this wouldn't have come without its own controversy.

Lewis Michaux was owner of National Memorial African Bookstore, the only black owned book store in Harlem. The older brother of Lightfoot Solomon Michaux, a pioneer in the world of televangelism acted as an advisor for U.S. President Harry S. Truman and helped to build a 500+ unit housing development for the poor, and cousin to Oscar Michaux, one of the first ever black filmmakers. Lewis Michaux was a pillar of the Harlem community, and his book store was viewed as a mecca for African-American intellectual enlightenment. He was married to Bettie Kennedy Logan and they had one son.

Lewis Michaux was born in Newport News, Virginia in 1895. Michaux had little formal education and before migrating to New York he worked as a pea picker, window washer and deacon in Pennsylvania. Lewis Michaux went on to open *African*

National Memorial Bookstore

National Memorial Bookstore in 1932 on 7th Avenue. The store became an important reading room of the late 1950's and 1960's of the Civil Rights Movement. and was found to be a rare place for black people and black scholars interested in learning more about black anything. Michaux stimulated a generation of students, intellectuals, writers and artists. He called his bookstore "House of Common Sense and the Home of Proper Propaganda". Michaux's bookstore had over 200,000 texts and was the nation's largest on its subjects.

Michaux was active in the black nationalism movement from 1930s to the 1960s and supported Marcus Garvey's Pan-Africanism. Harlem had been the headquarters of Garvey's Universal Negro Improvement Association and African Communities League of the world – the largest mass black movement of the times.

Understandably, Michaux was upset that Dr. King wasn't doing the signing at his store, especially considering that Blumstein's didn't even sell books and had also developed a reputation for treating black employees poorly.

In 1885 Louis Blumstein arrived in the United States from Germany. He worked as a street peddler and in 1894 opened a store on Hudson Street. In 1898 he moved to West 125th Street between Seventh and Eighth Avenues, already a major regional shopping center. Blumstein later died in 1920 and in 1921 his family demolished the store for a five-story building, the biggest thing on 125th street after the Hotel Theresa, at Seventh Avenue.

When Blumstein's rebuilt its store, blacks were expanding the base they had established in Harlem early in the century. By the mid-30's they largely occupied a vast stretch of central Harlem going from 111th to 155th street, and from Madison to St. Nicholas Avenue.

Whites resisted black migration to Harlem housing, and it was no different with jobs. In the late 20's black religious and civil leaders began pointing out that 125th street merchants hired only or mostly whites which was the same Blumstein's Department Store. In 1929 Blumstein's did hire its first blacks, but only as elevator operators and porters.

In 1932, one leader, J. Dalman Steele, called for a boycott of such companies, but his call was ineffective. In the spring of 1934, as more New Yorkers lost jobs because of the Depression, the Rev. John H. Johnson, vicar of the Protestant Episcopal St. Martin's Church, began a "Buy Where You Can Work" campaign. The New York Age newspaper backed this movement noting that 75 percent of Blumstein's sales were to blacks but that it refused to hire black clerks or cashiers.

In 1934 The Citizens' League For Fair Play plastered the streets with fliers that read "Refuse to Trade with L.M. Blumstein 230 West 125th Street" and "This firm, acknowledging its large proportion of Negro business, has refused to employ Negro Clerks. Stay out of Blumstein's! Refuse to buy there!" The League's economic boycott was supported by more than 50 churches and groups. Among those churches was the Abyssinian Baptist Church pastored by both Adam Clayton Powell, Sr. and Jr. The boycott's theme was "Don't Buy Where You Can't Work" and turned out to be highly successful. Not only did Blumstein's change their hiring practices; their department store was the first to use black mannequins and, no doubt a shock to some white shoppers, a black Santa Clause at Christmas time.

So, perhaps due to Michaux's sometimes controversial view on race relations, the signing was scheduled at Blumstein's anyway. This wouldn't be the last time Dr. King heard from Lewis Michaux.

Averill

The timing of the whole trip couldn't have been more perfect. Democratic incumbent Governor William Harriman and Republican challenger Nelson Rockefeller were in the midst of an intense political battle and both believed that the "negro vote" could be the key to victory. A massive rally was scheduled to be held on September 19, 1958 at 7th Ave. and 125th street, in front of Harlem's legendary Hotel Teresa.

In the 1940's and 1950's, Hotel Theresa became a center of the social life of the black community of Harlem; it was then that it became known as "the Waldorf of Harlem." The hotel profited from the refusal of prestigious hotels elsewhere in the city that refused to accept black guests. As a result, black businessmen, performers, and athletes were thrown under the same roof. In 1960, Fidel Castro came to New York for the opening session of the United Nations, and, after storming out of the Hotel Shelburne on Lexington Avenue in Midtown Manhattan because of the management's demand for payment in cash, he and his entourage stayed at the Theresa, where they rented 80 rooms for $800 per day.

Besides Dr. King and the two politicians, also scheduled to speak at the rally was Bayard Rustin's mentor and NAACP president A. Phillip Randolph.

Baseball great Jackie Robinson delivered the opening remarks while Harlem Icon Duke Ellington conducted his orchestra below the stage. Then Baseball slugger Robinson began the event with a fiery rhetoric that would set the tone for the entire rally. "We are the balance of power. We can put Governor Harriman back in office or we can put Mr. Rockefeller in. I'm sure these two gentlemen realize the tremendous potential of you and me." Conspicuously absent from the proceedings was Harlem Congressman, Adam Clayton Powell Jr. Next up was Mr. Randolph, who must have made the two gubernatorial candidates very uneasy when he commenced a

long political attack on President Eisenhower for his admittedly
his lack of commitment to
lacking effort in regards to the civil rights movement.

After Harriman and Rockefeller each finished their individual
remarks, it was finally time for Dr. Martin Luther King Jr. to
speak. However, as he approached the lectern with his prepared
speech, two very different kinds of hecklers began berating him
for all to hear. The first was Lewis Michaux, who along with 12
supporters, made his feelings about the book signing snub very
clear. His protest echoed what he said to a reporter after the
event. "I've been here for twenty-two years as the leading Negro
bookstore in Harlem, and yet King and his publishers didn't
even come to see me!" Dr. King tried to ignore Michaux and
continued his remarks. "Many of you had hoped I would come
here to bring you a message of hate against the white man
because of what has happened. I come with no such message.
Black supremacy is just as bad as white supremacy." King stated.

As he said these words, another heckler began to make
herself heard in the crowd, voicing hatred for all Caucasians and
any Negro who cooperates with them. Despite the ruckus, Dr.
King soldiered on with his speech. "I come with a message of
love rather than hate. Don't let any man make you stoop so low
that you have to hate. Have love in your hearts for those who
do you wrong." King finished. The crowd surprisingly erupted
into applause, drowning out the verbal vitriol of the heckler.
After the event, the idea of a bodyguard for King was discussed
within his inner circle, but he quickly dismissed it, deeming it all
to be an isolated incident. Little did he know that the second
heckler who had berated him would go on to change his life
forever the very next day. Her name... Izola Ware Curry.

Figure 13: Hotel Theresa in 1950's

Figure 14: Stanley David Levison, a white Jewish Communist

A.L. Cohen

Figure 15: Lewis H. Michaux inside his bookstore, African National Memorial Bookstore: 1895-1976 – Credit Wikipedia

Figure 16: Lewis Michaux's House of Common Sense and Home of Proper Propaganda, 1964 - Credit Corbis Image courtesy of Betrman

4 THE LIFE AND TIMES OF IZOLA WARE CURRY

Izola Ware was born on June 14, 1916 in Adrian, Georgia located in Emmanuel and Johnson counties were the 1.4 square mile town had a population of 740 circa in the 1920 census. The daughter of sharecroppers, Izola was the seventh of eight children. In 1922, her father Mose Ware left his wife and children which caused them to gradually grow apart. Izola was only six years old when this happened.

Izola was born during the Great Migration Era from 1910-1930. Life was no crystal stair for blacks living in the early 1900's like the Ware family. The Great Migration was the traveling of approximately 6 million blacks from the South to other parts of America such as the Northeast, Midwest and West. From 1910 to 1970, African Americans left many southern states, primarily Mississippi, Louisiana, Texas and Alabama. By the 1970's blacks had largely transitioned from being in rural areas to becoming urbanized and more skilled. More than 40% of blacks had left southern rural areas for city areas, and 7% settled in the Western states.

Like many blacks, Izola left school in the 3rd grade at the age of 12 to enter the work force. Records also show that in 1937, at the age of 21, she married a man named James Curry. A marriage which ended six months later.

After her marriage dissolved, Izola fled to New York City but kept the last name Curry. It was during this time she started experiencing bouts of hysteria. Little did Izola know she was suffering from paranoid schizophrenia. The Ware family was no stranger to mental illness. It proved to be a generational curse on the women of her family. In a community where no one knew how to help you, the common option was to just lock you away. Even though Izola was aware that the others around her were sick it wasn't something she could detect in herself. Izola would frequently say that she was the "onlyiest Ware that had any sense."

Izola's aunt, Lucy Ware, suffered from schizophrenia before Izola was even born. Lucy is quoted frequently saying to her sister, Mattie "Look at those little people walking there." For eight years of her life, she was committed to an insane asylum in Milledgeville, Georgia. Izola's youngest sister, Georgia Wilson also suffered from severe mental illness and spent nearly a decade committed to the same psychiatric facility. It is said that she recovered and later moved to New York to live with relatives.

In 1948, Izola's 21-year old nephew was electrocuted for kidnapping a white woman during a 1916 prison break. The generational curse of violence and mental illness had a stronghold on the Ware family. It was an unfortunate trend that ran deep and it was slowly grabbing hold of Izola. It would be exacerbated by the passing of her mother in 1949.

Izola had a reputation for disappearing and mysteriously reappearing without much explanation. She sought work in various parts of the country, from Georgia to Florida to New York City. Family events such as the commitment of her youngest sister to an insane asylum and the death of her mother would bring her back into the family fold from her secret, obscure life.

1949. Izola's brother Luther Ware was quoted saying, "She started talking that random talk about four years ago... I remember last year when she was down here visiting from New York she said, 'I going back and kill me a man. I gonna kill me a man!' I said, "Girl, what the matter with you? What you talking about? And she said, 'Oh ain't nothing wrong with me. I just gets that way sometime.'"

In the 1950's, relatives reported that Izola had begun to hallucinate more about imaginary people and complained that "over amorous men" had begun to chase her, causing jealous women to plot against her. She frequently confided in her brother Luther of her hallucinations. "I been finding voodoo stuff (dead birds) under my pillow. I'm going to find somebody to help me." Izola decided that she would fight the magic that was being done against her with her own black magic.

In 1956, Izola visited her lover, Scottie Mumphrey in St. Louis. "I ain't crazy," Izola exclaimed after Mumphrey suggested that she seek professional help. She continued to live in St. Louis for two months as her mental bout grew. Cleo Allen, Scottie Mumphrey's brother in law, recalled Izola once asked his wife to cook dinner for her. She waited until dinner had been prepared and said that she was going to the bathroom. She instead left the house and returned the next morning. That same day, Izola quickly packed her bags and left for New York.

Throughout her childhood and into middle age years, Izola would work for white employers whom would frequently fire her. They didn't like her, so she thought. Once in New York she found employment as a domestic worker and began dating a

Harlem musician named Leroy Weekes, who eventually asked her to marry him. Izola refused. Supposedly, Weekes had ties to the NAACP which deeply upset her.

At this point, her mental health had begun to rapidly deteriorate. Her delusions and paranoia made it difficult for her to stay employed. This began the strange chapter of her life that saw Ms. Curry bounced around from job to job including brief stints in Cleveland, St. Louis, Charleston, Savannah, Miami, Daytona Beach, Lexington, and Columbia. In March, 1957, while working in Daytona Beach, Florida, she put a down payment of $1.00 on a .25-caliber, Italian automatic at a pawn shop and later returned to pick it up paying the balance of $26.84. During this time she also began writing a letter to the FBI claiming that communist agents were out to get her.

Upon returning to New York in 1958, Izola lived with her nephew, Reverend Edward Jackson in Inwood, NY. While being interviewed, he recalled an incident of Izola pulling out a realistic looking cigarette lighter pistol from her purse. He recalls the incident to investigators, "She held us in a corner for 20 minutes saying she would shoot us if we moved. Then she pulled out a cigarette, lit it with the lighter and started laughing hysterically." Soon after this stunt was pulled, her nephew forced Izola to move.

Izola then began living in a rented room in Harlem at 121 West 122nd street. The windowless five dollar a week room only measured 6 by 12 feet. To her neighbors, Ms. Curry was a mystery. A supremely antisocial woman. She spoke with a distinct southern accent that often made her words unintelligible.

However, her landlady, Mrs. Agnes Skeeter never noticed any

real problems. She recanted in a newspaper article, "Mrs. Curry didn't give me no trouble. On Saturdays when I went to collect the rent and she wasn't there, she come to my house and pay me." It almost seemed to matter who Izola was talking to!

Perhaps her most distinguishing quality was her audacious fashion sense, a style that leaned heavily on expensive cat eye glasses and large bold earrings.

Figure 17: Izola Ware Curry9.20.1958 - Credited NYT

Figure 18: Izola Ware Curry 9.20.1958 - Credit Worthopedia

Figure 19: Izola Ware Curry 9.20.1958 - Credited Associated Press

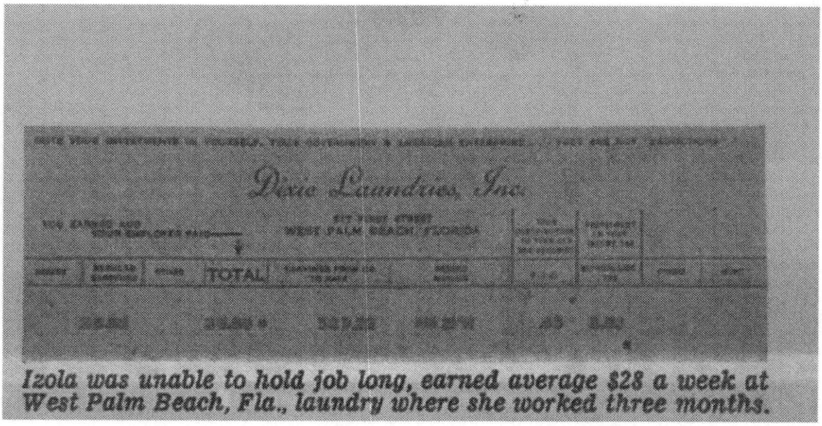

Figure 20: Izola's pay stub from Florida - Credit Jet Magazine 1958

Figure 21: Izola's two brothers, Luther and Thomas Ware and sister
Bertha Irvin Ware - Credit Jet Magazine 1958

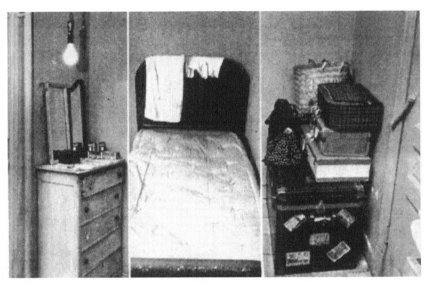

Figure 22: Izola's Room in Harlem, NY which measured 6x12 feet – Credit Jet Magazine 1958

5 WHEN TWO WORLDS COLLIDE

On the day of Dr. Martin Luther King Jr.'s book signing at Blumstein's, Izola wrote a letter to Scottie Mumphrey, a sweetheart of hers from St. Louis. The letter indicated how unhappy and unwell she truly was. It read in part, " Listen I tell you what you do. Please get me a job before I get there please. I know what I am talking about. It is these peoples in this house that is doing it. She married to an old black guy and they are trying to keep me here. One, go to Florida. If I do come your peoples is going to Florida, and they go it fix on that end... I am so disgusted I don't know what to do. An in this little room am no one to talk to."

That afternoon, Izola left home with voices in her mind. She carefully packed an approximately seven inch letter opener also known as a Japanese pen knife and a .25 caliber pistol that she had purchase in a Florida pawn shop for $27.84.

It was 3:35pm on Saturday, September 20, 1958 in Harlem, New York. Dr. King sat in the shoe section of Blumstein's Department Store to autograph copies of his latest book, *Stride Toward Freedom: The Montgomery Story* as part of his lecture tour. Dozens of people anxiously stood in the line including 20 Harlem school children from Wadleigh Junior High School. This school exemplified the post-war struggle for African American educational opportunity inside all levels of municipalities that undermined it. The Wadleigh teachers had to be innovative, bringing them to pick up on varied strands of contemporary and also

historic educational activism which helped them face the challenges of underfunding and persistently low test scores. The 20 students selected not only were given the privilege to attend the book signing, but the opportunity to meet a great civil rights leader on the rise which would forever impact their lives. who

Also, standing in line anxiously were officials from the National Association for the Advancement of Colored People (NAACP), city officials and civic leaders. Many blacks had resented Dr. King for holding his book signing at a Jewish department store instead of the ONLY black owned and operated book store in Harlem, *National Memorial African Bookstore.*

Izola stood in line, dressed in a white blouse, blue skirt and a plastic raincoat. She could have continued to stand in line but in her mind there was no time for that! Dr. King was busy signing books and taking pictures with the community's elite and the media, such as Jack Blumstein, the owner of Blumstein's Department Store, James Watson & Robert Johnson, both editors of Jet Magazine.

According to witnesses, there were about 50 people in front of Izola when she gathered with those who were looking to have their books signed by Dr. King. Her level of anxiety would not allow her to remain in place as needed to get to the front of the line. After wading through the crowd, Izola approached Dr. King and asked him, "Is this Martin Luther King?" He replied, "Yes it is", all the while assuming she was another fan. As she forcefully approach him Izola shouted, "You made enough people suffer in the last six years!", then she whipped out the letter opener and viciously stabbed Dr. King in the chest. He never saw it coming!

Mass hysteria erupted in the department store as the instantaneous reality set in that Dr. King had been stabbed. The sharp thinking of a bystander knocked Izola's hand away from the letter opener before she could stab again. She started to run but was quickly apprehended by individuals in the crowd, while being heard screaming, "I've been after him for six years. I'm glad I done it!" In the midst of the scuffle, out comes a loaded .25 caliber pistol from her bosom.

Still seated, Dr. King remained calm and collected, as the letter opener protruded from his chest. Vernoll Coleman, a freelance photographer at the book signing stated, "I hadn't realized he was stabbed until I saw the instrument sticking out of his chest." Even in his midstream of distress, Dr. King said, "That's all right. That's all right. Everything is going to be alright."

At approximately 3:38pm a call went into the NYPD as Izola stood calm in the midst of all the chaos. She didn't even try to escape, just stood there with a weird peace and no remorse. Izola was detained by two of Blumstein's security guards, Clifford Jackson and Harry Dixon with absolutely no resistance as they waited for the NYPD to arrive. Still, with no resistance, back straight, head cocked back and NO HANDCUFFS, two NYPD Police officers escorted her out of Blumstein's. She was then quickly hustled into a cab and taken to the hospital where Dr. King identified her as his assailant and received a medical evaluation. Later that evening she was transferred to the 28th precinct on 123rd street.

Figure 23: Dr. King before his actual book signing on September 20, 1958 - Credit Vernoll Coleman

Figure 24: Students from Wadleigh Junior High School meeting Dr. King - Credit The New York Times

Figure 25: Dr. King Stabbed in the chest with a Letter Opener - Credit Vernoll Coleman / New York Daily News

Figure 26: Izola in police cab after stabbing Dr. King brutally with a letter opener - Credit Getty Images

Figure 27: Izola being escorted to car after stabbing Dr. King – Credit Associated Press

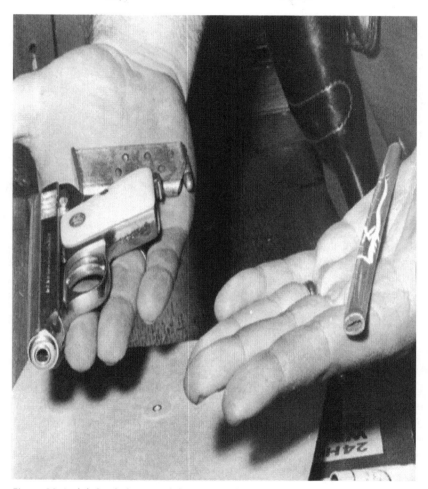

Figure 28: Izola's loaded gun and the case to the letter opener she used to stab Dr. King - Credit Associated Press

6 THE INTERROGATION

"You should have let that Nigga die!", said the desk sergeant at the precinct as Izola calmly strolled in escorted by two officers.

Who was Izola Ware Curry? Where did she come from? Why was she in Harlem? Then the most perplexed question of them all would be: Why was she trying to kill Dr. Martin Luther King Jr.?

After arriving at the 28th precinct Izola was held in an interview room as officers gathered at the observation window. Whispering amongst themselves with looks of confusion and astonishment, "Is this the woman?" "Is this the woman that stabbed Dr. King?"

As the interrogation began, lead by Assistant District Attorney, Howard A. Jones. the line of questioning seemed endless but in heated watts, it shed a spotlight on how mentally disturbed this woman truly was.

TRANSCRIPT
An official account of the interrogation of Izola Ware Curry.
Date: Saturday, September 20, 1958
Place: 28th Precinct located on 123rd Street in Harlem, New York
Time: 9:45pm to 11:20pm
Whom: Interviewer: Assistant District Attorney, Howard A. Jones |

Mr. Jones: What is your name?
Izola: Izola Curry.
Mr. Jones: And are you married or single?
Izola: Separated.
Mr. Jones: And you was married?
Izola: I were married.
Mr. Jones: What is your husband's name?
Izola: James Cury.
Mr. Jones: What was your name before you got married?
Izola: Ware.
Mr. Jones: Where is James Cury now?
Izola: In Savannah.
Mr. Jones: Georgia?
Izola: Right.
Mr. Jones: How long have you been separated?
Izola: About twenty years.
Mr. Jones: And where were you married?
Izola: I'm not saying that all these things no, all these things was not running through my mind this afternoon. I'm basing this on the facts that before that this came down, I'm following the story down but you know I'm saying that this could have had something – evidently she had this in mind before bring to me to start you know. Let me slow down and make it a little easier for you. In other words I want to say that maybe she was put there for the simple reason to catch me and after she got the goods on me, evidently maybe she could- thought I would be a

good speaker, a good campaigner or something, that's what I am trying to bring out. But this afternoon have no bearing on that.

Mr. Jones: I see. The story was you wanted to get away from.

Izola: When she to me "you'll never get away with the information that you got." Now, if you want to ask me what was the funning threw my mind, now I'll answer that question.

Mr. Jones: Answer that question.

Izola: Yes. Because when she told me you'll never get away with it because the NAACP will never get away, that was running threw my mind and I never had any peace to that day till this.

Mr. Jones: When did you find out that Dr. King was going to be at Blumstein's this afternoon?

Izola: Well, I didn't find out I didn't find out. I'll answer that I didn't find out I passed there last night on my way to the movies and it was such a mob up there I had to miss who – even the band was playing, so I said what is the commotion.

Mr. Jones: This was last night?

Izola: Yes.

Mr. Jones: Whereabouts?

Izola: On 125th street and 7th Avenue

Mr. Jones: And what sort of mob was it?

Izola: Was just people.

Mr. Jones: Was there a speaker?

Izola: I didn't stop, I kept going.

Mr. Jones: About what time?

Izola: I say on the – what time? Well I saw all the show so I guess it was (witness pauses) well, the last I said around seven something.

Mr. Jones: Between seven and eight?

Izola: That's right.

Mr. Jones: That's when you passed 7th avenue and 125th street?

Izola: That's right

Mr. Jones: And you saw this mob of people?

Izola: Yes,

Mr. Jones: And heard the music and heard a band?

Izola: That's right.

Mr. Jones: Did you ask somebody what's going on?

Izola: They said it's this King man. He's here. Arthur King you know, he's going to speak or something. What's his first name? What's his name? Arthur King or Arthur Lucer or something? He's a doctor King I understand.

Mr. Jones: I thought he was a Reverend. *she thought his name was Arthur*

Izola: That's right Reverend and all that in there with it.

Mr. Jones: Do you know his first name?

Izola: Arthur, Arthur I believe.

Mr. Jones: And was anything said last night that would connect this doctor with the NAACP?

Izola: I said I went straight to the movies.

Mr. Jones: Well, do you know this Dr. King does socialize with the NAACP?

Izola: He is the leader of it.

Mr. Jones: And at any rate, you didn't stop at this rally last night, this meeting on the street?

Izola: No, I kept on.

Mr. Jones: What movie did you see?

Izola: I went to the movie here on 125th street.

Mr. Jones: And you saw the picture there?

Izola: Yes.

Mr. Jones: Do you recall what the picture was?

Izola: Was Tarzan and something, but – anyway Tarzan; And the other picture was, I recall that one, it was a native picture.

Mr. Jones: After the picture you went home, is that right?

Izola: I did

Mr. Jones: And you --

Izola: No, after the picture show I did not go home I met a friend of mine and I stood up and talked a good while.

Mr. Jones: Where did you meet this friend?

Izola: 110th and 7th Avenue. And I met him. I stood there and talked with him a while an went to bed.

Mr. Jones: 110th and 7th Avenue.

Izola: That's right.

Mr. Jones: What's this friend's name?

Izola: Smittie.

Mr. Jones: Where does Smittie live? Do you know?

Izola: No, I didn't even ask him. It's a man I didn't bother I just see him whenever and talk to him.

Mr. Jones: And do you know his full name?

Izola: No I don't. I just know him for about 20 years and I couldn't tell you his last name. But I know he's from Florida.

Mr. Jones: Florida?

Izola: Yes.

Mr. Jones: And he lives around the neighborhood someplace?

Izola: Yes.

Mr. Jones: Does he live on Lennox or in the Bronx?

Izola: As I said, I don't know.

Mr. Jones: You talked to Smittie for a few minutes and then you went home, Is that right?

Izola: Yes.

Mr. Jones: What time did you leave the house today?

Izola: Well, I said around three or quarter to three. Around three, or somewhere around that.

Mr. Jones: Where were you going?

Izola: I went shopping.

Mr. Jones: Where did you shop?

Izola: I went on 125th street, looking around. And on 7th Avenue.

Mr. Jones: Where were you going to shop?

Izola: I wasn't shopping at any particular store.

Mr. Jones: Just window shopping?

Izola: Yes.

Mr. Jones: Had you bought your groceries, is that what you were shopping for?

Izola: No, I wasn't picking up any groceries. I was picking up little items.

Mr. Jones: Now, you were going to 125th street, shopping along the way as you walked, is that right?

Izola: Yes

Mr. Jones: And you passed Blumstein's?

Izola: Yes.

Mr. Jones: Now, do you want to tell us what happened in Blumstein's?

Izola: Well, I shopped around there in Blumstein's for a good while, and some – So, finally, this doctor whatever you might call him, King came in and I walked up to him and I said you have been annoying me for a long time trying to get this children, I have no objection of you getting them in the schools at all, but why torture me, why torture me I'm no help to him by him killing me don't mean after all Congress is signing anything. By torturing me don't mean congress is going to sign, I can still get a blood clot from this aggravation today. After that day congress isn't going to sign anything and I'm just dead.

Mr. Jones: What did he say?

Izola: I was drunk in my head. I don't know what he said. He looked up at me and what he said, I don't know.

Mr. Jones: Then what happened?

Izola: Then I hit him with this paper opener.

Mr. Jones: You had this paper opener?

Izola: Yes I did.

Mr. Jones: Where did you have it?

Izola: In my bag?

Mr. Jones: And is that your paper opener?

Izola: Yes, it's my paper opener – letter opener...

Mr. Jones: And what did you do with that letter opener?

Izola: That, he has it (indicating).

Mr. Jones: But when you pulled it out of your bag at Blumstein's, what did you do with it, tell us what happened?

Izola: I just told you. I hit him with it.

Mr. Jones: Where did you hit him? What part of his body?

Izola: I didn't even look to see.

Mr. Jones: Why did you hit him with the paper opener?

Izola: Because after all if it wasn't him it would have been me, he would have killed me.

Mr. Jones: Was he sitting down at the desk when you did this?

Izola: Yes, He was autographing books.

Mr. Jones: Did you buy a book?

Izola: No. I didn't.

Mr. Jones: Was there a line standing at the desk?

Izola: No. There was not. A lot of people standing around, It wasn't no line.

Mr. Jones: And is this the letter opener that you had? (indicating)

Izola: Yes. That's the letter opener.

Mr. Jones: Has that been marked? Will you scratch the initials

Detective Belmar: My Initials?

Mr. Jones: Yes. What are your initials?

Detective Belmar: J.B.

Mr. Jones: And you have scratched those initials into that letter opener?

Detective Belmar: Yes.

Mr. Jones: Go one. Tell us what happened after that.

Izola: Well, The police grabbed me, and took me and handcuffed me.

Mr. Jones: I believe later on somebody scratched you. Is that correct?

Izola: Well, when they grabbed my bad my bag flew out of my hand and my wallet and everything went all over the floor. Now, they didn't stop to pick it up, they was so busy pushing me so, wait a minute - - - I don't follow that answer that again?

Mr. Jones: What I am referring to specifically is the gun. I believe a gun was found on you.

Izola: Yes, that's right.

Mr. Jones: Is that your gun?

Izola: Yes, it is.

Mr. Jones: And is this the gun here? (indicating)

Izola: That's right.

Mr. Jones: For the record, the serial numbers appear to bell7163. I's a Cal. 635 make in Italy. The mark appears to be ANLT.ARMI.GALESI.BRESCIA.AMDG. It's an automatic pistol, white handle and bone handle and there is an A on the handle. Is there a - - - there a mark with the lettering A.B., and a sort of monogram and initials A.B., standing for Ptl. Buancore, Anthony

11114 28th Sqd. Are those your initials you scratched on it?
Ptl. Buancore: Yes sir.
Mr. Jones: Is that the gun officer that you took from the witness here?
Ptl. Buancore: Yes, sir.
Witness: Now the FBI knows I have it.
Mr. Jones: Mrs. Curry, where did you get this? (indicating)
Izola: Daytona Beach.
Mr. Jones: And you bought it?
Izola: Yes.
Mr. Jones: When did you buy it?
Izola: About a year ago.
Mr. Jones: And how much did you pay for it?
Izola: Twenty Six Dollars.
Mr. Jones: Was it loaded when you had it today?
Izola: Yes, It was.
Mr. Jones: And do you know how to shoot and load it?
Izola: They showed me. The woman showed me in the store in the store. I Never had one in my hand.
Mr. Jones: Let the record show there is a clip and seven bullets here. All are the same size. For the record, one of them S-E-R-N-dask U-M-C 25 automatic. Did you buy the bullets when you bought this gun?
Izola: These are the ones right there. (indicating)
Mr. Jones: You bought these when you bought it in Daytona Beach?
Izola: Yes.
Mr. Jones: And are these the bullets that were in the gun today?
Izola: That's right.
Mr. Jones: You put them there?
Izola: Yes, they have been there ever since it was loaded.
Mr. Jones: And you have never taken these bullets out of this gun?
Izola: No. And I never took the gun out of the house either.
Mr. Jones: You took it out today, is that right?
Izola: Yes.

She'd never taken out the gun before and left sales clip "?

Mr. Jones: This is the first time you took it out of the house since you bought it?

Izola: That's right.

Mr. Jones: Well, why did you take it out today?

Izola: Because after all I haven't got a job and what in the world I'm going to do for a living, with their pulling me off the job every day and I'm to to work and their trying to force me to make me drop my head to drink either become a prostitution, and I'm not being either one.

Mr. Jones: And what were you going to do with the gun today?

Izola: I was going to protect myself if some of these member attach me. Because I know his members are you know, following him.

Mr. Jones: You mean Dr. King?

Izola: That's right.

Mr. Jones: Reverend King?

Izola: Yes.

Mr. Jones: And you expected trouble from some of his followers today?

Izola: I figure they would be.

Mr. Jones: What makes you think there would be trouble today?

Izola: I'm just thinking that after all sure, some of them there was no thinking at all, after all a man in his power I would say after all he was people following him, they would probably try to protect him.

Mr. Jones: You felt they might bother you, is that right?

Izola: That's right.

Mr. Jones: You said they have bothered you before?

Izola: Definitely.

Mr. Jones: Do you want to tell us who they are now?

Izola: I'll save the rest of the story for my lawyer. I won't to the F.B.I. and after all I think they should give me a lawyer. I have reports direct to the F.B.I. and also I reports to the President of the United States, and I've also been to the President six times with this case.

Mr. Jones: Which precinct?

Izola: Up here not this precinct the court, served summonses
Mr. Jones: Did you get the summons against anybody?
Izola: Yes I did, I got it against this Leroy Weeks, the one I wants picked up with Francis Kravish.
Mr. Jones: Leroy Weeks is one of the people?
Izola: Yes, he's in it.
Mr. Jones: Where does he live?
Izola: 54 Lexington Avenue.
Mr. Jones: When was the last time he bothered you about this?
Izola: Well the last time I saw her and him about - -, no, I saw her him since I saw her.
Mr. Jones: When did you see him?
Izola: I would say about around, that's about approximately three years to.
Mr. Jones: When was the last time you got summonses against Weeks in the Magistrates' Court?
Izola: Well, I got about six against him and more than that.
Mr. Jones: When was the last time?
Izola: Last time I would say around, I'd say about a year ago, two years ago between then, but I got about six summonses on him more.

```
Statement of:              Izola Cury.

Made to:                   Howard Jones, ADA.

Date:                      September 21, 1958.

Time:                      9:45 p.m. to 11:20 p.m.

Place:                     28th Precinct, New York City.

Appearances:               Det.Belmar Sh.#1259 28th Sqd.
                           Det.Hickey Sh.#1767 Man.East Ho
                           Sgt.Harding Sh.#800 28th Sqd.
                           Ptl.Buancore Sh.#1114 28th Sqd.
                           Mr. Herman Chief Homicide Buroa
Stenographer:              Joseph J. Renda.
- - - - - - - - - - - - - - - - - - - - - - - - - - - -
BY MR. JONES:

    Q    What is your name?

    A    Izola Cury.

    Q    And are you married or single?

    A    Separated.

    Q    And you was married?

    A    I were married.

    Q    What is your husband's name?

    A    James Cury.

    Q    What was your name before you got married?

    A    Ware.

    Q    Where is James Cury now?

    A    In Savannah.

    Q    Georgia?

    A    Right.

    Q    How long have you been separated?

    A    About twenty years.

    Q    And where were you married?
```

Figure 29: Page one of Interrogation Report

Date of Report_____

TO: ALEXANDER HERMAN   From: Asst. D. A. _____ Howard A. Jones

Time and Place of Injury: 3:30 P.M., Sept. 20, 1958, main floor Blumstein's Dept. Store
                           230 W. 125 St.

Manner of Injury: Stabbed - center chest

Place Statements taken

Police Officers Assigned:

28 Squad

Ptl. Anthony Duane #114 - 28 Pct.
Det. James Belmar #1260 - 28 Squad
Det. Edward Kelly #2398 - M.E.H.S.

INJURED

Name: Rev. Martin Luther King   Marital Status and Age

Home Address:

Business Address and Occupation:

Time and Place of death:

DEFENDANT

Name: Izola Ware Curry

Home Address: 121 W. 122 Street, Top floor

Business Address and Occupation: Domestic - unemployed

Marital Status and Age   42 - separated

Arrested or Other Disposition: Arrested

SUMMARY OF FACTS

Rev. King was in Blumstein's Department Store autographing copies of his
newly published book. Defendant entered the store, asked "Is that Luther
King?" Then she walked up to desk where King was seated, stabbed him with
letter opener which she took from her purse. When searched later,
defendant was found to be carrying concealed a fully loaded Italian make
automatic. Questioning of defendant revealed her to be quite emotionally
disturbed. Committed to Bellevue on 9-21-58.

Figure 30: Original Case Report for Izola Ware Curry 9/22/58

Committed to Bellevue 9/21

53

Figure 31: Izola In Police Station - Credit Associated Press

*Figure 32: Izola Ware Curry at Police State after brutally
stabbing Dr. King – Credit Associated Press / Corbis*

Figure 33: Izola Ware Curry in Police Station, 9.20.1958 – Credit Associated Press

Figure 34: Izola Ware Curry inside the Police Precint 9.20.1958

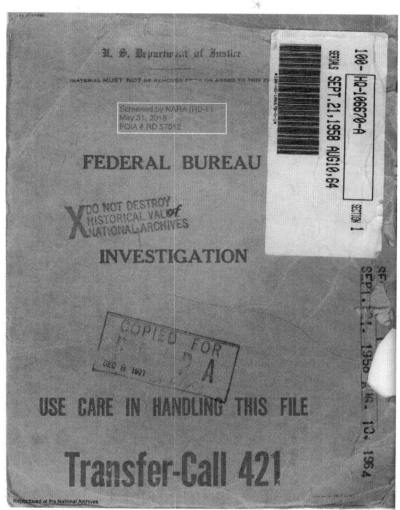

Figure 35: Credit - Federal Bureau of Investigation

Figure 36: Credit - Federal Bureau of Investigation

Figure 37: Credit - Federal Bureau of Investigation

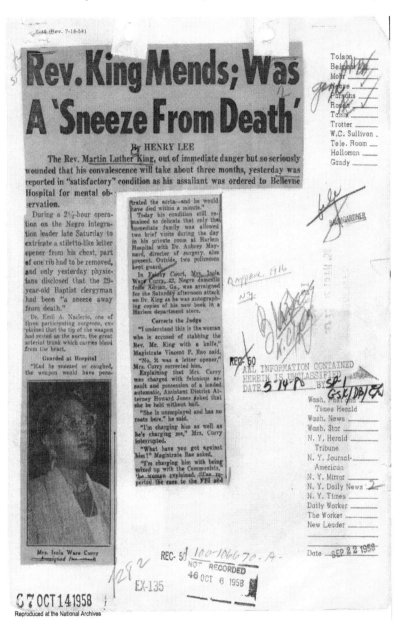

Figure 38:Credit - Federal Bureau of Investigation

Figure 39: Credit - Federal Bureau of Investigation

7 CONSPIRACY THEORY

In a Psychiatric report that dates October 22, 1958, Doctors Theodore Weiss and John Cassity wrote, "This defendant has been under constant observation at this institution since September 21, 1958. While usually cooperative and complacent in the routine ward procedures, she has been prone to become very excited and agitated. During these episodes, she is very demanding and has at times threatened to affect her escape, Also, it was noted that she has become threatening and assaultive." It goes on to read, "This behavior is occasioned by her delusional ideas that people are persecuting her. The delusional system seems to have had its origin about 5 years ago, when she developed the idea that the members of the NAACP were all communist and that they had been instrumental in and had been obstructing her from obtaining and retaining employment and that they had made scurrilous remarks about her. She confesses that many of those whom she accuses of persecuting her, she does not know personally. She has moved about in many states of this country in order to avoid her persecutors, but without success. She believes she has been under constant surveillance and all her movements are known to the NAACP and Dr. King. She has feared for her life and for the past year has been carrying a gun to protect herself against possible assault."

THE COMMUNIST PARTY

Appreciation is not necessary in order to accept the fact that the Communist Party had a presence in the civil rights movement. Historical records indicate that there were many of this party that worked toward justice: racially, economically and politically. Whether they were independent societal contributors or collaborators is when the account becomes varied. Communist believe that the most productive resource is society, by which all of those efforts should be shared publically, under the control of the government. This is understood to be the best way to prevent over consumption by a select, prepare for war and to maintain a stabilized economy. Some would say that this system is a breeding ground for inequality; being that the rationing of compensation on all levels is left up to like minds or one mind (dictatorship).

During the Great Depression the communist position internationally was that African-Americans in the South have the right to self-determination: basically meaning they had the right to build their own nation as other black communist were doing around the globe. Sounds good but still a very sensitive concept to comprehend with value. The African American population remained heavily concentrated in the South, where exclusion and oppression under Jim Crow laws remained a plague. The South was and would continue to experience segregation and inequality that was based on race alone, decades after the Great Depression. This was not the prevalent face of disparity internationally as freedom had more liberties in places such as Canada.

The Communist Party USA was founded in America with blacks having no association to it. The minority representation was mostly non-fluent English speaking, European immigrants formerly a part of the Socialist Party; which had no contact with blacks other than those competing with them for jobs and housing. It would make sense that this group of individuals would have looked to the Communist Party after the split as many in the Socialist Party USA were still not totally against racism. Even though socialism was built on the concept of a society owned and regulated economic system; most socialist were not outwardly against racism. Whereas the Communist Party USA had begun to take a stand in support of civil rights by the 1930s.

The Marxian class theory was partly written by Karl Marx, a German philosopher, economist and socialist, known as the Father of Communisms in 1848. The theory asserts that an individual's position within a class hierarchy is determined by his or her role in the production process, and argues that political and ideological consciousness is determined by social economical position (class).

In 1953, Dr. Martin Luther King Jr. called communism "one of the most important issues of our day". As King rose to prominence he frequently had to defend himself against allegations of being a Communist, though his view that "Communism and Christianity are fundamentally incompatible" did not change. Although sympathetic to communism's core concern with social justice, King complained that with its "cold atheism wrapped in the garments of materialism, communism provides no place for God or Christ" In his 1958 memoir, he reported that although he rejected communism's central tenets, he was sympathetic to Marx's critique of capitalism, finding the "gulf between superfluous wealth and abject poverty" that existed in the United States morally wrong. Writing his future wife, Coretta Scott, during the first summer of their relationship, he told her that he was "more socialistic in my economic theory than capitalistic. And yet I am not so opposed to capitalism that I have failed to see its relative merits".

With Dr. King's own words to his wife, it should be of no surprise that he and Stanley Levison found common ground. Stanley Levison, being a white non practicing Jew, was a well-known communist in support of the civil rights movement. The FBI also took a heightened interested in Levison in 1959 when they learned of Levison's connection with King and the movement. FBI chief J. Edgar Hoover believed that Levison was a communist agent, and that through Levison's international communism influenced King's actions. In the fall of 1963 The FBI received authorization to proceed with wiretapping from Attorney General Robert F. Kennedy and informed President John F. Kennedy, both of whom unsuccessfully tried to persuade King to dissociate himself from Levison.

For his part, King adamantly denied having any connections to Communism, stating in a 1965 Playboy interview that, "there are as many Communists in this freedom movement as there are Eskimos in Florida". Dr. King also claimed that Hoover was "following the path of appeasement of political powers in the South." President Hoover's concern about communist infiltration of the civil rights movement was meant to "aid and abet the salacious claims of southern racists and the extreme right-wing elements." In that same interview, King advocated that blacks and other disadvantaged Americans be financially compensated for "historical wrongs."

In 1950, out of a total population of 1.5 million Americans, 50,000 were communist. Tired of oppression and capitalism, Americans began to believe that communism would be a better system for society and allow for greater opportunity and equality for citizens. This was against the wishes of the American government and planted the seeds for what is now considered "government" surveillance. What was viewed as government loyalty boards began to investigate what publications federal employees read and what civil unions and civic organizations they belonged to. Actors and directors in

Hollywood became blacklisted for their political beliefs and ordinary citizens such as doctors, lawyers and social workers lost their jobs for being suspected of supporting communism. These events took a major toll on Izola Ware Curry to the degree that she felt within herself that she had to be responsible for eliminating who she thought would be the cause of this uprising which was Dr. Martin Luther King, Jr.

The turn of the 20th century would bring consistent decades of challenges for America and subsequently blacks in America. Take your pick of obstacles from the Great Depression, Cold War, Ku Klux Klan, Jim Crow laws, racism and modern day slavery. Even though these obstructions would prove to be obvious; the presence of the Communist Party and Civil Rights Movement had the opportunity to actually be beneficial. Sooner than later this mid-century relationship would prove to be a hindrance as the American people detested communism and it was no secret how they felt about the Civil Rights Movement.

The "black belt" of the south had been deemed the poorest of the nation and it was home to mostly African American communities. The *black belt* was a region of the United States that described the prairies and dark fertile soil of central Alabama and northeast Mississippi. During the 19th century the land was developed for cotton plantations based on enslaved African American labor. The term would became associated with these conditions and its laborers.

The communist would use any opportunity to fight against social and economic issues regarding a classism system. They took on unemployment which landed them in the pit of the "black belt" with suffering blacks. The New Deal era was bringing unions and the Communist Party sought to be in this growth. Whether it was a need for more jobs, legal advocacy, the right to vote and/or to be a juror; the communist party was attracted to blacks. They were the population disproportionally affected by these disparities due to their race. The communist were against racism, however they knew that being involved with the civil rights movement could prosper the labor movement expeditiously---blacks needed work.

CIVIL RIGHTS MOVEMENT & NAACP

The Civil Rights Movement became a cornerstone of the Communist Party's platform in the United States, and actively courted black intellectuals and leaders in an attempt to appeal to African-Americans. The communist knew moving forward on their mission inclusive amongst blacks would almost be impossible without the NAACP. Their motives were questionable even though it appeared they were after the same goal of equality. In 1937, the Communist Party members decided to join the NAACP, because they believed that it was important for them to be united. The membership of the NAACP grew drastically, but no communist held any sort of leadership position within the group. The people were more educated and held better jobs then a lot of the people that were in the Communist Party. Also, many of the African American communists would not even attend the NAACP meetings, because the NAACP believed the meetings to be for a higher class of people in which they were not. If they did attend, the communist element felt as if they were not taken seriously, and many of them grew frustrated and lost interest in the group.

The International Labor Defense was the first to offer its assistance in the Scottsboro Boys case. William L. Patterson, a black attorney who had left a successful practice to join the Communist Party USA, returned from training in the Soviet Union to run the ILD. After fierce disputes with the NAACP, with the ILD seeking to mount a broad-based political campaign to free the nine Scottsboro Boys while the NAACP followed a more legalistic strategy, the ILD won and took control of the defendants' appeals. The ILD attracted national press attention to the case, and highlighted the racial injustices in the region.

The Scottsboro Boys were nine African American teenagers, ages 13 to 20, falsely accused in Alabama of raping two white women on a train in 1931. The landmark set of legal cases from this incident dealt with racism and the right to a fair trial. The case included a lynch mob before the suspects had been indicted by, all-white juries, rushed trials, and disruptive mobs. It is commonly cited as an example of a miscarriage of justice in the United States legal system.

The greater questions would be, Why would Izola Ware Curry, a socio-economically disadvantaged service worker, be against integration and an equal standard of living for not just African Americans, but all Americans?

From her lengthy questioning session with Assistant D.A. Howard Jones, Izola admitted that she had been following the career of Dr. King and had been greatly affected by his social and racial impact. Izola made it no secret that she was against integration and the potential influence of communism and the NAACP in the African American community.

A public consensus about Izola Curry's state of mind quickly hardened into a judicial conclusion. She was declared insane. She attacked King, she believed, because he was oppressing her. He had led troubling boycotts against whites, and worse, He was a communist. These same beliefs were commonly held by many whites. Though many bigoted whites no doubt quietly cheered the stabbing, it seemed reasonable to conclude that a black woman sharing white prejudices was insane because she was black. When James Earl Ray, who was a white man, that was accused of killing Dr. King was arrested He not considered to be insane.

THE WHITE CITIZENS COUNCIL

It has been a theory for decades that The White Citizens Council was instrumental in the attempted assassination of Dr. Martin Luther King Jr., and was responsible for the successful assassination of lawyer and civil rights icon Medgar Evers. Medgar Evers, who's first assignment from the NAACP was to interview Mississippi residents who had experienced intimidation from the WCC and prepared affidavits for evidence against them. He was subsequently assassinated on June 12, 1963 by Byron De La Beckwith, a WCC member and the KKK. The WCC paid all of Byron's expenses and he was acquitted by an all-white male jury. In 1994 he was re-tried by a jury of 8 black and 4 whites who found him guilty of murder. Byron was sentenced to life in prison where he later died in 2001 from heart trouble.

After the stabbing of Dr. King, the White Citizen's Council provided monies for the defense of Izola Ware Curry. As Izola sat in Bellevue awaiting trial, the monies that came in for her defense gave rise to speculations that they were behind her attempted assassination plot. The White Citizens Council (WCC) was an American white supremacist organization formed on

July 11, 1954 in an effort to keep the Deep South segregated and maintain the aggression and oppression of blacks across the United States. After 1956, it was known as the Citizens' Council of America. With about 60,000 members, mostly in the South, the group was well known for its opposition to racial integration during the 1950s and 1960s, when it retaliated with economic boycotts and other strong intimidation against black activists, including depriving them of jobs. Their mission statement read, **"When in the course of human events, it becomes necessary to abolish the Negro race, proper methods should be used. Among these are guns, bows and arrows, sling shots and knives. We hold these truths to be self-evident that all whites are created equal with certain rights; among these are life, liberty and the pursuit of dead niggers."**

In normal white supremacist fashion, one of the letters Dr. King received while in the hospital recuperating was one of hate. It came signed from "White Voting Citizen Mississippi" expressing regret that the accused attacker, Izola Ware Curry "didn't finish the job."

OFFICIAL PSYCHIATRIC REPORT:

In a Psychiatric report dated October 22, 1958 the doctor wrote, "This defendant has been under constant observation at this institution since September 21, 1958. While usually cooperative and complacent in the routine ward procedures, she has been prone to become very excited and agitated. During these episodes, she is very demanding and has at times threatened to affect her escape, Also, it was noted that she has become threatening and assaultive." It goes on to read, "This behavior is occasioned by her delusional ideas that people are persecuting her. The delusional system seems to have had its origin about 5 years ago, when she developed the idea that the members of the NAACP were all communist and that they had been instrumental in and had been obstructing her from obtaining and retaining employment and that they had made scurrilous remarks about her. She confesses that many of those whom she accuses of persecuting her, she does not know personally. She has moved about in many states of this country in order to avoid her persecutors, but without success. She believes she has been under constant surveillance and all her movements are known to the NAACP and Dr. King. She has feared for her life and for the past year has been carrying a gun to protect herself against possible assaults. Since her admission here, she has threatened to sue certain newspapers regarding their account of the instant offenses, which she feels was completely justified, this, despite the fact that she had had no personal relationship with the victim of her assault. It is quite evident that her conscious thinking is dominated by her delusional ideation to the extent that she is incapable of having an understanding of the charges against her or of making a defense thereto. Consequently, the undersigned believe that this defendant is a suitable case for further observation and treatment in a state mental hospital."

The trial of Izola Ware Curry was described as "hasty". On October 17, 1958, Dr. King testified on her behalf with a great amount of forgiveness and concern for her. Upon hearing Dr. King's testimony, Izola was indicted for attempted murder in the first degree. After hearings following this indictment, Izola was adjudicated incompetent to stand trial and was therefore committed to the Mattaewan State Hospital for the Criminally Insane.

Figure 40: Communists marching in the May Day parade in New York in 1935.CreditCreditDick Lewis/New York Daily News, via Getty Images

Figure 41: A packed hall in 1947 for a speech by Eugene Dennis, a longtime leader of the Communist Party in the United States .Credit Patrick A. Burns/The New York Times

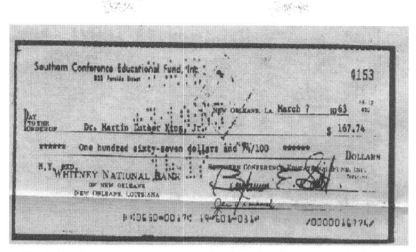

Figure 42: Above is a Photostat of an SCEF (Southern Conference Education Fund) check to King signed by Dombrowski and Benjamin Smith, who was a registered Foreign Agent for Fidel Castro. - Credit Jesus_is_savior.com

Figure 43: Credit Alamy Stock Photo

Figure 44: Credit ICP.org

Figure 45: Credit Federal Bureau of Investigation

8 TRIAL AND VERDICT

COURT OF GENERAL SESSIONS
COUNTY OF NEW YORK

THE PEOPLE OF THE STATE OF NEW YORK
-against-
IZOLA WARE CURRY, Defendant

THE GRAND JURY OF THE COUNTY OF NEW YORK, by this indictment, accuse the defendant of the crime of AN ATTEMPT TO COMMIT THIS CRIME OF MURDER IN THE FIRST DEGREE, committed as follows:

The defendant, in the County of New York, on or about September 20, 1958, willfully, feloniously, intentionally and with a deliberate and premeditated design to effect the death of Martin Luther King, attempted to kill said Martin Luther King by willfully and wrongfully striking him with a knife.

Frank S. Hogan
District Attorney

November 8, 1958

Hon. Abraham N. Geller
Judge, Court of General Sessions
100 Center Street
New York 13, N.Y.

Honorable Sir:

Re: Izola Ware Curry

    The attached report of the formal hearing in the case of
Izola Ware Curry, by the qualified psychiatrist appointed by
the Director (Physician-in-charge), Bellevue Psychiatric
Hospital, is respectfully submitted.

Very truly yours,

Arthur Zitrin, M.D.
Director

November 7, 1958

Re: Izola Ware Curry

REPORT OF FORMAL HEARING HELD ON NOVEMBER 6, 1958

Pursuant to an order by the Hon. Abraham N. Geller, Judge of the Court of General Sessions, dated October 24, 1958, directing that a formal hearing be held in the case of the above named defendant in accordance with the provisions of the Code of Criminal Procedure, such formal hearing was held in the Psychiatric Division of Bellevue Hospital on November 6, 1958, by the two qualified and designated psychiatrists signing this report.

Prior to the hearing, the referees' oaths, in triplicate, also the designation signed by Dr. Arthur Zitrin, Director (Physician-in-charge) Division of Psychiatry, Bellevue Hospital, New York City, appointing the two qualified psychiatrists, were filed in the office of the Clerk of the Court of General Sessions.

The following were present at the hearing: Patrolman Anthony Buancore, Shield No. 1114, 29 Precinct, Manhattan, Dr. Theodore S. Weiss, qualified psychiatrist, Bellevue Hospital, Dr. James Reilly, qualified psychiatrist, Bellevue Hospital.

SUMMARY, CONCLUSIONS AND RECOMMENDATIONS.

In compliance with an order signed by Hon. Abraham M. Geller, Judge of the Court of General Sessions, County of New York, directing that a formal hearing be held in accordance with the provisions of the Code of Criminal Procedure, such hearing was held at the Psychiatric Division of Bellevue Hospital on November 6, 1958, in the case of the above named defendant, who was carefully examined in a joint conference held by the two qualified psychiatrists signing this report.

Patrolman Buancove stated that when he apprehended the defendant she had emerged from the store in Harlem where she had stabbed Rev. King; that she did not resist arrest and kept repeating the phrase "He took away my freedom. He and NAACP were after me. This has been going on for the last 5 years. It's a frame-up and I lost job after job because of them" He further stated that the defendant did not appear to be intoxicated at the time.

At this hearing the defendant presented approximately the same picture as that described in our report to the Court of October 22, 1958, namely, she gave expression to fairly systematized, bizarre and delusional material. She stated that for at least 5 years she felt that the NAACP was causing her to lose her jobs, causing her annoyance, taking away her freedom and that the Rev. King had a part in the entire conspiracy against her. Defendant is confused, her speech was disconnected dissociated. She gave expression to paranoid delusions into which she had no insight. Judgment was nil.

In conclusion, and as a result of this formal hearing and joint psychiatric examination, it is the opinion of the two qualified psychiatrists signing this report, that Izola Ware Curry at the present time is in such a state of insanity that she is incapable of understanding the charge, proceedings or indictment against her or of maker defense; that she is suffering from schizophrenia of the paranoid type and is potentially assaultive and dangerous. And that she is a suitable case for commitment to Matteawan State Hospital.

Theodore S. Weiss, M.D.   James   Reilly, M.D.

Qualified Psychiatrist   Qualified Psychiatrist

Bellevue Hospital   Bellevue Hospital

Sworn to before me this
7th day of November, 1958

Anne M. McCarthy
Commissioner of Deeds
New York County Clerk No.
Commission Expires June 16, 1959

HIGHLIGHTS OF THE FORMAL HEARING

Following her police interrogation, Curry was quickly committed for observation at Bellevue Hospital's psychiatric ward. While "usually cooperative and complacent" on the ward, Curry was prone to getting agitated and excited. "During" these episodes, she is very demanding and has at times threatened to affect her escape. Also, it was noted that she has become threatening and assaultive," according to a psychiatric report.

Curry was diagnosed as a paranoid schizophrenic by two psychiatrists who reported that she had an IQ of 70, "low average intelligence," and was in severe "state of insanity." Assistant District Attorney Howard Jones asked that she be held without bail explaining that Ms. Curry was being charged with felonious assault and possession of a loaded automatic. "I'm charging him as well as he's charging me," Ms. Curry interrupted him. "What have you got against him?" Magistrate Rao asked. "I'm charging him with being mixed up with communists," Izola explained.

"I want a lawyer from the state!" Izola Stated. "This woman is ill," Rao said. "I'm not ill!" Ms. Curry answered sharply. When asked if she had a lawyer, she said "Yes, his name is Herman!" As she was led away she shouted that the lawyers name was Sanford or Stanford, her words being too difficult to understand.

A Manhattan judge would later concur with the psychiatrist's conclusion that Curry who had been indicted for attempted murder – should be committed to the Matteawan State Hospital for the Criminally Insane but not before being corrected by Izola. "I understand this is the woman who is accused of stabbing the Rev. Mr. King with a knife," Magistrate Vincent P. Rao said. "No, it was a letter opener," Ms. Curry corrected him! Magistrate Vincent P. Rao died in 1993 of Parkinson disease at the age of 79.

On November 17, 1958, two months after stabbing King, Curry – described as a "forty-two year old colored female" in hospital records –arrived at Matteawan, where the most famous patient was George Metesky, the "Mad Bomber: who had been arrested and institutionalized the prior year for a 16-year bombing spree across New York City.

Upon admission to Matteawan, Curry showed no remorse for attacking King. The psychological report states that "This patience fluctuates between occasional fairly logical thinking and very confused illogical thinking." She remained "generally suspicious, seclusive and resentful of correction. She is nasty and abusive at times," noted officials in a clinical summary. At times, Curry was thought to be heard responding to voices in her room. Once, she spoke of killing someone there, saying, "The S.OB. Rev. King ought to be here."

In an interview with hospital staff, Curry denied that "anybody put her up to" harming King. The stabbing, Curry said, "was entirely her own idea," according to a Matteawan report.

Figure 46: Bellevue Hospital 1950 – Credit Wikipedia

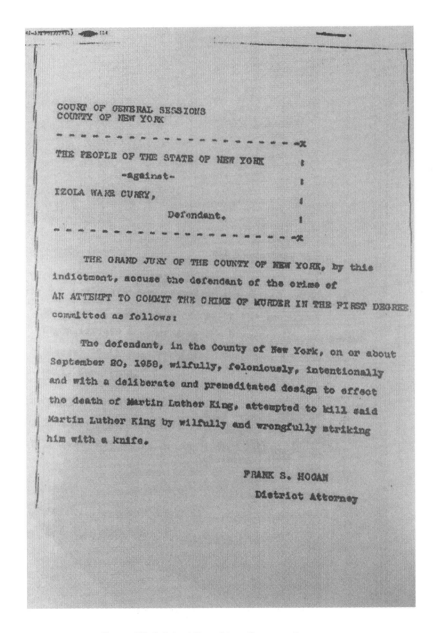

Figure 47: Original Grand Jury Document

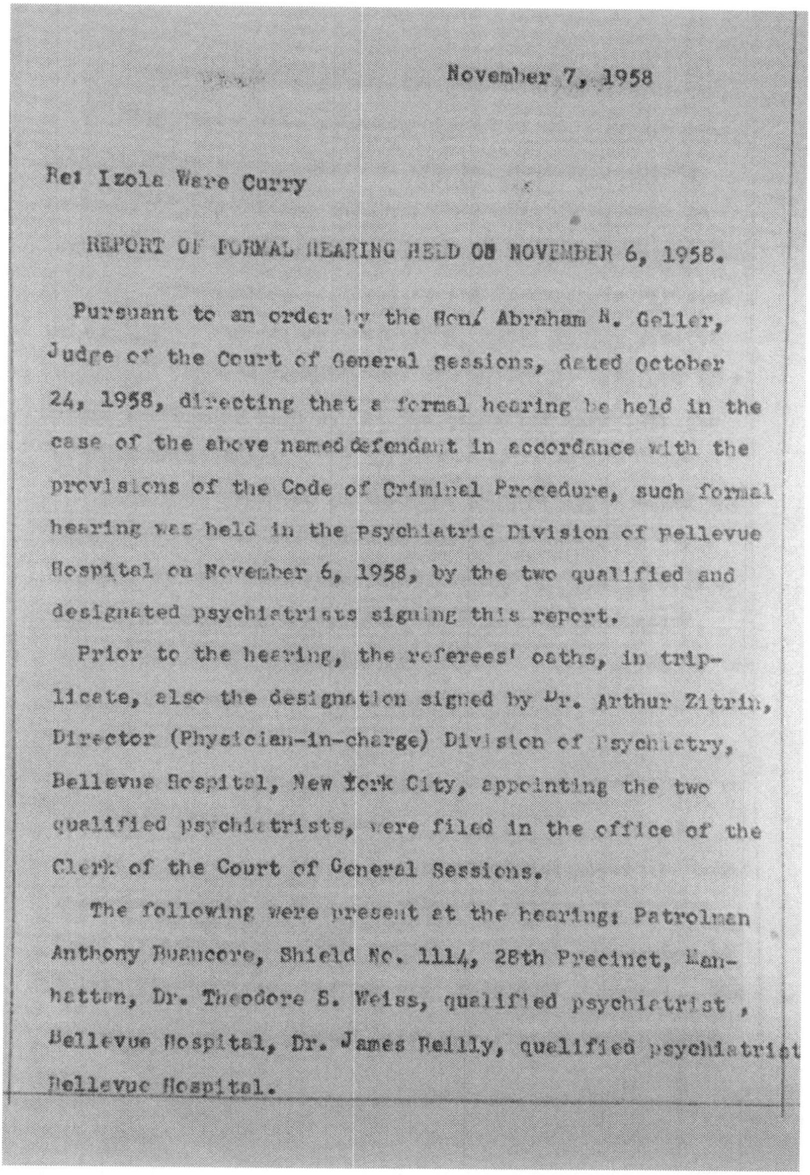

November 7, 1958

Re: Izola Ware Curry

REPORT OF FORMAL HEARING HELD ON NOVEMBER 6, 1958.

Pursuant to an order by the Hon. Abraham N. Geller,
Judge of the Court of General Sessions, dated October
24, 1958, directing that a formal hearing be held in the
case of the above named defendant in accordance with the
provisions of the Code of Criminal Procedure, such formal
hearing was held in the psychiatric Division of Bellevue
Hospital on November 6, 1958, by the two qualified and
designated psychiatrists signing this report.

Prior to the hearing, the referees' oaths, in trip-
licate, also the designation signed by Dr. Arthur Zitrin,
Director (Physician-in-charge) Division of Psychiatry,
Bellevue Hospital, New York City, appointing the two
qualified psychiatrists, were filed in the office of the
Clerk of the Court of General Sessions.

The following were present at the hearing: Patrolman
Anthony Buancore, Shield No. 1114, 28th Precinct, Man-
hattan, Dr. Theodore S. Weiss, qualified psychiatrist ,
Bellevue Hospital, Dr. James Reilly, qualified psychiatrist
Bellevue Hospital.

Figure 48: Original Formal Medical Report from Bellevue Hospital

Re: Izola Ware Curry

SUMMARY, CONCLUSIONS AND RECOMMENDATIONS.

In compliance with an order signed by Hon. Abraham N. Geller, Judge of the Court of General Sessions, County of New York, directing that a formal hearing be held in accordance with the provisions of the Code of Criminal Procedure, such hearing was held at the Psychiatric Division of Bellevue Hospital on November 6, 1958, in the case of the above named defendant, who was carefully examined in a joint conference held by the two qualified psychiatrists signing this report.

Patrolman Juancove stated that when he apprehended the defendant she had emerged from the store in Harlem where she had stabbed Rev. King; that she did not resist arrest and kept repeating the phrase "He took away my freedom. He and the NAACP were after me. This has been going on for the last 5 years. It's a frameup and I lost job after job because of them."

He further stated that the defendant did not appear to be intoxicated at the time.

At this hearing the defendant presented approximately the same picture as that described in our report to the Court of October 22, 1958, namely, she gave expression to fairly systematized, bizarre and delusional material. She stated that for at least 5 years she felt that the NAACP

Figure 49: Original Formal Medical Report p.2

86

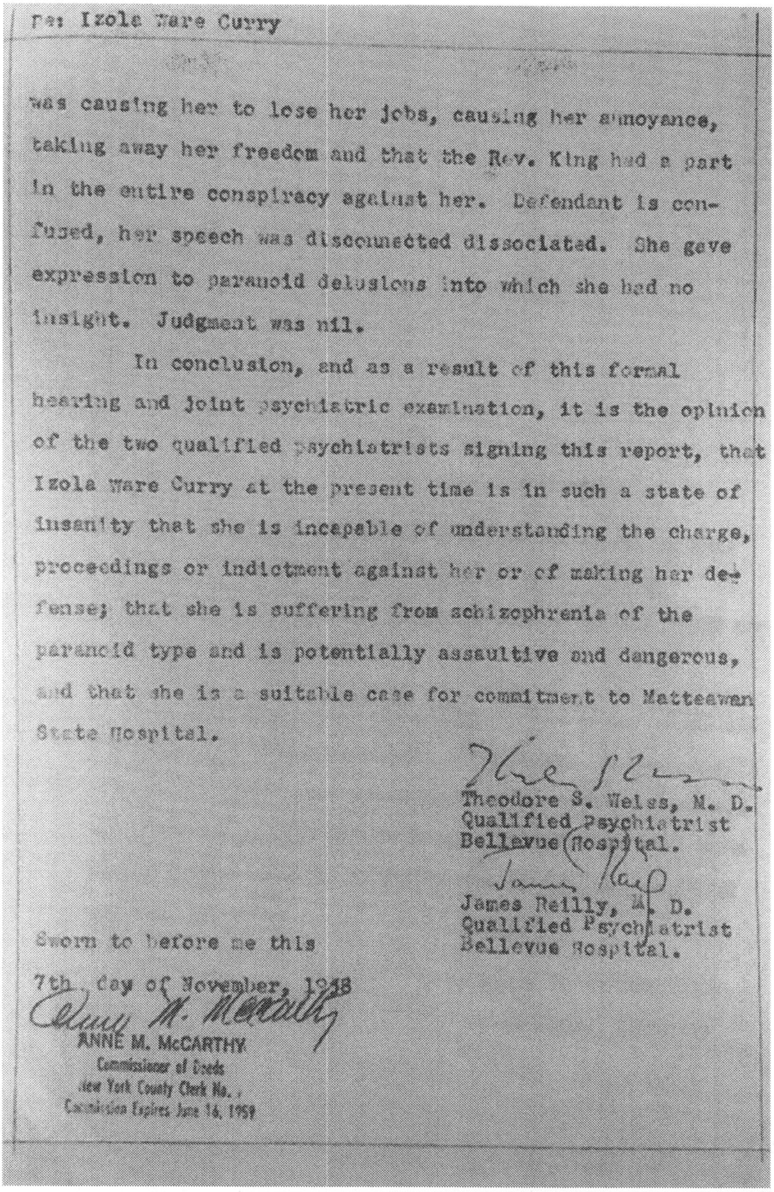

re: Izola Ware Curry

was causing her to lose her jobs, causing her annoyance, taking away her freedom and that the Rev. King had a part in the entire conspiracy against her. Defendant is confused, her speech was disconnected dissociated. She gave expression to paranoid delusions into which she had no insight. Judgment was nil.

In conclusion, and as a result of this formal hearing and joint psychiatric examination, it is the opinion of the two qualified psychiatrists signing this report, that Izola Ware Curry at the present time is in such a state of insanity that she is incapable of understanding the charge, proceedings or indictment against her or of making her defense; that she is suffering from schizophrenia of the paranoid type and is potentially assaultive and dangerous, and that she is a suitable case for commitment to Matteawan State Hospital.

Theodore S. Weiss, M. D.
Qualified Psychiatrist
Bellevue Hospital.

James Reilly, M. D.
Qualified Psychiatrist
Bellevue Hospital.

Sworn to before me this

7th day of November, 1958

ANNE M. McCARTHY
Commissioner of Deeds
New York County Clerk No.
Commission Expires June 16, 1959

Figure 50: Original Formal Medical Report pt.3

9 THE INCARCERATION OF A CRIMINAL IN CUSTODY

GUILTY AS CHARGED

We are often held as a prisoner incarcerated physically behind mental bars, in a state of confinement, when the real convict is our thoughts and mental state that influence our natural behaviors.

Thoughts that blackmail us, threatened us, intimidates us, and pressure us, to carry out behaviors in and through our physical bodies. Our mental state can sometimes become a victim, and it becomes victimized by its environment often times, now subject to take on and embrace certain philosophies and concepts that will dictate our mode and movements.

There are more imprisoned people sitting on the outside of a prison than there are sitting on the inside of a prison-imprisoned by concepts, philosophies and ideologies that they believe are the gospel.

MATTEAWAN STATE HOSPITAL

The notion of a psychiatric facility, for many, brings to mind ideas of padded rooms and strait jackets. Working in the medical field, I can assure you that it's no walk in the park. It's unlike most stereotypes you've heard or seen. Upon admission, your required to check all baggage except the emotional variety for inspection. You're not allowed to have things like belts, shoelaces, drawstrings on hoodies or sweatpants. Patients were not allowed to have any images that appeared to be violent, or anything sharper than a dull pencil.

For 80 years, Matteawan State Hospital was one of the nation's most famous institutions for the "furiously mad." In 1886, the state had purchased 246 acre Date Farm in the village of Matteawan for $25,000. It was the perfect location to relocate New York's first asylum for the Insane Criminals, which opened in 1859 on the grounds of Auburn. This asylum would receive convicted persons who became mentally ill. The asylum was severely overcrowded and the patients were often "doubled up" making no room for expansion.

The new site in Matteawan was accessible by rail, offered good tillable land, pure water and had pleasant scenery between the Hudson River and the Fishkill Mountains. The state hired an architect to draw out plans for a building with "an abundance of light and ventilation" and the ability to accommodate 550 patients. In April 1892, the Asylum for the Insane Criminals relocated their 261 patients from Auburn to Matteawan.

Matteawan State Hospital functioned the same as the state's civil hospitals except for tighter security. Doctors prescribed the program of "moral treatment" developed in the early 1800's. It consisted of kind and gentle treatment in a stress-free, highly routine environment. Patients who were capable were assigned to a work programs (often called "occupational therapy"): cooking, maintenance, farming, making baskets, rugs, clothing and bedsheets.

Patients were given outdoor exercise in the courtyards twice daily and motion pictures were shown weekly. Radios and phonographs were available as well as a vast variety of recreational activities such as tennis, handball, chess and cards. By 1949, new treatments had been added to the traditional moral treatment (now called "milieu therapy"). Electric and insulin shock treatments were now being used extensively. Hypnosis and group therapy were also employed.

Since Matteawan's opening, the proportion of chronic and dangerous patients who could never be released steadily rose, and so did the hospital count. While the capacity gradually increased to about 1,000, overcrowding still continued. In 1959, there were nearly 1,500 men and 250 women. It was originally intended to house patients deemed too chronically dangerous for civilian institutions.

Through the 1960's, the facility operated under loose regulation guided by the whim of the superintendent, who determined at his judgement if a patient was fit to be release regardless of the severity of the crime.

In 1977 New York closed Matteawan and converted it into the Fishkill Correctional Facility, a security prison for men. The closing of Matteawan and its re-purposing as a prison signaled the criminalization of mental illness – a wholesale shift away from considering mental illness a medical condition amenable to treatment, toward punishment of persons who are afflicted. Today, Fishkill holds more than 1,500 male criminal offenders and is housed in an open dormitory-style housing typical of medium and minimum security prisons.

On March 30, 1972 Izola Ware Curry was transferred to Manhattan Psychiatric Center on Section 662B (730). The Manhattan Psychiatric Center is a New York-State run psychiatric hospital on Wards Island in New York City. The building strongly resembles that of the Creedmore Psychiatric Center in Queens.

SPINNING OUT OF CONTROL: ALLYNE SPINNER

Upon moving to her new home at Manhattan Psychiatric Center, Izola was assigned to a young Jewish social worker named Allyne Spinner. This was Ms. Spinner's first job in 1971 after graduating from Columbia University where she received her Masters of Social Work (M.S.W.) and became a trained, individual and group psychoanalyst.

With only one year's experience, she was given the responsibility of not just Izola Ware Curry, but all the other patients that were on that ward. At this time, the state had developed and implemented the "Family Care Program". This is a residential service sponsored by the Office of Mental Health for persons who have been diagnosed with serious mental illness. This program places individuals in need of community placement (residents) with persons certified to deliver residential care in their own homes. Before placement into the Family Care program, The mental health of patient's were evaluated. Allyne's job was just that, to evaluate if Izola and the other patients were competent to live in a societal environment. At first, she did not know about Izola's background, she just saw her as another patient on that ward. It wasn't until she read Izola's chart that she would realize who she was and the heinous crime that she had committed.

Izola's demeanor, according to Allyne was, a tall, attractive, classy, well dressed and very aloof woman. She stood out from the rest and was calm, effect blunt and not too interested in life. Almost depressed! This could have been due to the medicine, because the anti-psychotics blunted the affect. This was one of the side-effects of the medication according to Ms. Spinner.

Izola never wanted to talk about her assassination attempt on Dr. Martin Luther King Jr. She acted like it never happened. "This is part of the illness" Ms. Spinner exclaims. "Part of the trauma that she must have experienced."

"The attempt on Dr. King was the schizophrenia, the voices that told her to do it, and the paranoia that the NAACP was after her." As Allyne describes and emphasizes that the demeanor that she saw in 1972 was from the trauma. "The trauma of being arrested, being caught at doing something that she thought was correct. The voices told her to kill him, or whomever she was acting on behalf of."

Allyne goes on to explain that usually schizophrenia develops in the 20's, but when she met Izola she was 57, and when she tried to kill Dr. King she was in her 40's. It is Allyne's opinion that she must have been suffering from this illness for over 20 years. Either no one knew about her illness, or it just went untreated. It would also be her opinion, that it is possible that there could have been a group of white people in the South who used her to be the fall guy due to her state of mind. It's also possible in Allyne's opinion that her psychosis was fueled by the number of times in which she heard that Dr. King was a trouble maker. "With her being an unemployed domestic worker it's possible that Izola believed the NAACP was after her."

Allyne goes on to say that schizophrenics use an element of reality in their delusion. She believes it is possible that is how Izola muttered up the courage to do such a thing. They usually have some kind of reality to their psychosis and people took advantage of that.

Izola was being assessed by Allyne for the sole purpose of seeing if she was able, or well enough, to live outside of the hospital. We are made aware that because of Izola's particular status of being a "criminal insane patient" that she could never be discharged officially, but she could live outside of the hospital.

Figure 51: Inside of Mattaewan Insane Asylum: These pictures are taken in 2007 – Credits Rob Yasinsac

SOUTH INTERIOR COURT.

Figure 52: Credit - Revolvry.com

SOUTH FLANK PAVILIONS.

Figure 53: Figure 46: Matteawan State Hospital as it looked in 1913 - Credit Jeff Mcmullin

10 IZOLA WARE CURRY: A NEW LIFE

THE WALDEN CHRONICLES

In 1973, Izola Ware Curry was admitted to the "Family Care Program" where she was sent to live with the Walden family in Queens, New York. Izola believed that she was going to be of domestic help. Izola was so happy that she was finally going to be able to work again.

Mrs. Walden was a struggling single mother with three children. She had an older woman as her mentor who informed her of a state program, where she could have someone live in her home as part of an "adult adoption" program that would allow her to receive revenue, which she so desperately needed. She also had a lot of space in her Queens home which made her more comfortable with the thought of having someone stay with her and her children.

Mrs. Walden recants the first days that Izola Ware Curry came to live with her in her home. She said that she had no idea that Izola was the woman who committed the attempted assassination against Dr. Martin Luther King Jr. She recalls Izola as being a "refined little old lady".

Izola enters her new home for the first time after spending 14 years in the mental hospital. She came with a social worker whose name was Allyne Spinner who directly asked Mrs. Walden, "This is Izola and she is going to stay with you. Is that what you want?" Mrs. Walden replied, "Yes, that is what I want."

Izola toured the house and later said, "I would like to stay in the basement." They had a large basement. Mrs. Walden didn't think that was a good idea because she didn't want her hidden in the basement. She wanted her to be visible. Mrs. Walden then said, "That's not really available for you to live there, you will have to take one of the rooms upstairs." Izola responded, "That will be fine".

Mrs. Walden recants that although the social worker had not divulged the exact reason as to why Izola was incarcerated, that she did let her know that she had been sick for quite some time and just had no one to care for her. She informed Mrs. Walden that she just needed someone to care for her because she had no family or relatives and was well enough to be back in the general public and that she should have been out long before this placement. The social worker went to ask and make sure that Mrs. Walden was ok with having someone live with her that was in a mental hospital for 14 years.

We asked Mrs. Walden if she ever noticed any sign of mental illness, or any strange behaviors, or if anything had them worried. She responded by saying, "I didn't detect any mental illness but I watched her closely to see if I could pinpoint any abnormal behavior and I couldn't find anything. What I did find was that she was exceptionally clean, and I like that!"

Lynette Walden, the eldest daughter of Mrs. Walden remembers exactly how she and her family found out about Izola's crime, and how they confronted her. She recalls seeing a Jet magazine at school and was shocked to see the physical similarities between the Izola in the Jet magazine, and the Izola living in her home.

She went home and told her younger sister, Crystal what she had discovered at school. Of course Crystal did not believe her, but Lynette continued to hound and use that story from the Jet magazine to taunt her younger sister. One day, during an argument they were going back and forth and Lynette said, "I'm going to ask Izola if she did it!" Crystal became very disturbed and scared, not wanting Izola to remember or be triggered by this part of her history. Nonetheless Crystal was very curious and she went and asked Izola the daunting question.

"Izola, did you try and kill Dr. King? Izola responded to Crystal without even looking at her. She gazed straight ahead and said, "I never knew the man!" Crystal then went to tell her brother and sister again that Izola had stabbed Dr. Martin Luther King and it was true because it was in the encyclopedia, (showed them the picture of her). Crystal's brother said, "Well let me go ask her." But she would not allow that to happen for fear that he may hurt Izola's feelings.

Curiosity got the best of her, and she further went to approach her again saying, "Izola! Are you sure you never knew Martin Luther King?" she looked straight ahead, closed her eyes and said, "I never knew the man." This made Crystal a little upset for obvious reasons. She knew the truth and no one would believe her! To prove her point, Crystal went and brought the encyclopedia to her and said, "Izola, this is you right here in this encyclopedia." Izola never acknowledged it, nor did she say anything to that. She just sat there in silence with a gazed expression on her face.

The family decided that they were not to ask Izola anymore questions about her past. Mrs. Walden was very upset that she did not know nor had she been told about Izola's history. She immediately called Manhattan State Psychiatric Center and spoke to someone expressing her concerns and that she no longer wanted Izola to live with her. The lady on the phone said,

"We will come get her because if you don't want her to live with you anymore, we definitely won't leave her there." It would take two or three days before they would be able to pick Izola up.

During these few days the family was able to settle with the fact that yes, Izola had committed this crime. But the woman that was living in their home now was not the same woman. The woman that was living with them now was sweet, soft spoken, gentle, and funny.

"Whatever her problem was, she clearly did not pertain any of those same issues now, so I will just allow those skeletons to stay in her closet. Everyone has skeletons in their closets and this could have very well been anyone of us." said, Mrs. Walden

"That woman that stabbed him was not the woman that was living with me. Maybe she was set up, maybe there was more to the story. All that I know is that the woman living with me was NOT the same woman who stabbed Dr. King. We loved Izola and we took her for what she was. She was no threat to us and whatever happened was just a mistake." says, Crystal.

"Izola had an illness, and from where I sat with living and caring for Izola, that illness she overcame! Anyone who reads of Izola should realize that this is a person who at that time was out of control. And from that time deserves all the help, all the love, all the attention, and all the happiness that could be imparted onto her. She deserves it. She was a good woman" Mrs. Walden said. "I would like for people to understand, that once you have an illness, it does not have to be a lasting illness. I feel that people should not be stigmatized and treated with a long handled spoon just because they had an illness." Mrs. Walden

The Walden's truly believed that they were not harboring an attempted assassinator, or an attempted murder. They believed that they were helping someone to be a part of society without that stigma of what happened during a period of time when her mind wasn't even right. She was a regular everyday person to them.

The kids grew up and left the home of their mother, Mrs. Walden leaving her once really loud and busy home quiet and cold. She had met a man and decided to get married. With this came the unction to want to travel and enjoy the empty nester of a life that she had acquired.

She picked up the phone and called the hospital and stated that she no longer wanted Izola in her home. They said they would pick her up for her routine medical trip to the hospital which Izola did every few weeks. Mrs. Walden agreed but failed to tell Izola she was leaving for good. She had Izola get dressed for just the day in her best outfit because she was going to get picked up to go to the hospital for her routine check-up. The bus came and picked Izola up like nothing out the norm. This would be the last time Mrs. Walden or anyone else from the Walden family would see, hear or touch Izola Ware Curry.

Later that day, a nurse from the hospital come to pick up the belongings of Izola.

We have no idea how this could have affected Izola. Here it is she had finally found a family that accepted her, loved her and respected her. She had built a solid relationship with the Walden family, a feeling of security she had never felt. Izola would frequently attend church with the family in Queens, NY at Saint Auburns Deliverance Center. At times she would take the children to the corner store to buy snacks and treats all by herself. There were even times when the friends of the children would come over and they were introduced to Izola as being part of their extended family. She was actually part of the family living a normal everyday life. She was loved, talked

to, played with for the first time in her life. She had stopped taking meds four years prior because during the time of being with the Walden's she had no
incidents of hostility or aggressiveness and she was able to get along in the home and community. At this point her delusions were absent and that is one of the reasons she did not require psychotropic medication.

The Walden's knew that she had no family, so Izola was off to try and pick up the pieces on her own, but now with a some what sane mind.

Figure 54: The House Izola Ware Curry lived in after being released in the Family Care Program - Credit Wearica Walden

Figure 55: Wearica Walden, Crystal Walden & Dr. Jeff Gardere during a 2015 interview with producers of When Harlem Saved A King documentary

11 IZOLA WARE CURRY: THE LOST YEARS

On the eighth floor of a nursing home in Queens, New York a 98-year-old woman sits slumped in a wheelchair in the hallway outside her room. She is sleeping, oblivious to the roar coming from the television of her next-door neighbor, who is watching "The Price is Right" at an ear-piercing volume.

Though the corridor is uncomfortably toasty on this July morning, the woman has a knitted shawl over her shoulders. She is wearing green sweatpants, a green T-shirt, and black shoes with velcro closures. The remaining wisps of her hair are gray and tangled. In her clenched left hand is a wad of tissues that she will use to absent-mindedly dab at her face and rheumy.

As she naps in the hallway, it is hard to image that frail Izola Ware Curry was once a would-be assassin, a woman who nearly changed the course of U.S history with a seven-inch steel letter opener.

For more than half a century, Curry has lived in complete anonymity, despite the fact that she nearly murdered Dr. Martin Luther King Jr. in September 1958, a decade before the civil rights leader was struck down by James Earl Ray at the Lorraine Motel in Memphis.

After subsequently being found "in such a state of insanity" that she could not understand the attempted murder charge lodged against her (and, as a result, was incapable of aiding her defense), Curry was committed to the Matteawan State Hospital for the Criminally Insane in upstate Fishkill, New York.

Curry was 42 when she entered the state Department of Corrections facility. New of her commitment in November 1958, two months after she stabbed King – appeared in various newspapers, including The New York Times, which devoted three paragraphs to the development. It was the time Curry's whereabouts, or her condition, would be the subject of press coverage.

The Smoking Gun published some of the first documents about King's stabbing in 1998. They have intermittently tried to determine what became of the woman who nearly killed the civil rights leader. But checks of carious databases and a wide variety of public records – real estate property, telephone, litigation, auto registration, civil judgments, voter rolls, and driver's licenses turned up no trace of Curry (or anyone else named "Izola Curry")

It was not hard to conclude that Curry was deceased. Actuarially speaking, in fact, it seemed likely she had died, perhaps decades earlier. Still, no obituaries or death notices had ever been published for Curry. Also, her name never appeared in the comprehensive death index maintained by the Social Security Administration.

After she tried to murder Dr. King, Curry disappeared into the state's corrections/mental health system, apparently never to be heard from again. Until November 2014.

While again conducting an every-few years search for Curry, a TSG reporter discovered that an "Izola Curry" had registered to vote from a Queens Address three months before the 2012 presidential election. A copy of Curry's voter application form, obtained from the New York City Board of Elections, includes a Hillside Avenue home address and is stamped "NURSING HOME." Most importantly, the document also lists the voter's date of birth as June 14, 1916, identical to that of the "demented black woman" who tried to murder Dr. King.

Izola Ware Curry had been living in Queens, NY for about 40 years. While residing in predominantly African-American communities, she appears to have generated little, if any notice. Which is understandable, since the details of King's stabbing, let alone the name of his attacker, are largely lost to history. In fact, most Americans would be unable to name the man who actually succeeded in assassinating the civil rights leader.

Hillside Manor nursing home in Jamaica, Queens is a no-frills facility with 300 beds on bustling Hillside Avenue. The 98-year-old lived in a small room with a twin bed that looks out onto a rear parking lot. Next to her bed was a walker and a side table that appeared to hold the entirety of her possessions, a stack of books, a couple of framed photos, and a small pink stuffed animal.

During a recent visit, we found a snoozing Curry parked in a wheelchair outside her room at 11am. Ten other residents were similarly situated, scattered across the hallway in their wheelchairs. Some were sleeping, but all were silent.

When the 98-year-old Curry awoke, she greeted the interviewers with a smile. "Miss Curry loves to talk," offered a cheery attendant as she passed in the hallway.

During the 30-minute conversation, Curry spoke haltingly and, at times, mumbled answers that were hard to decipher. At one point, she directed her visitor to fetch a chair from her room so that he did not have to stand over her.

While Curry described her daily routine – up at 5:30am, bed around 10pm, and not much going on in between. She talked about how she ended up in the nursing home and met questions about King and stabbing with a furrowed brow and a blank stare. While offering no recollections of the attack, Curry referred to "1958" and said that she was placed that year in a "hospital for the criminally insane." However, a 1980 letter from the New York State Office of Mental Health provides some general details about Curry's term at Matteawan.

According to the letter, Curry spent nearly 14 years at the upstate New York facility before being transferred in March 1972 to the Manhattan Psychiatric Center on Ward's Island in upper Manhattan. She spent about a year there before officials placed her in the Rosedale, Queens home of a woman certified through the state's "Family Care" program to provide residential care for those diagnosed with mental illnesses.

At the time of the 1980 letter, a state psychiatrist reported, Curry had spent the prior seven years in "Family Care," a period during which "there have been no incidents of hostility or aggressiveness and she has been able to get along satisfactorily in the home and the community." Dr. Avram Finger added that Curry's delusions "are, at present, absent and she has not required psychotropic medication for the past 4 years." Additionally, following an examination by a panel of Manhattan Psychiatric Center

officials, Curry was judged to be "coherent, relevant, cooperative and no present danger to self or others." The letter went on to say that "she was examined on April 22, 1980 by the entire Hospital Privileges and Transfer Committee of Manhattan Psychiatric Center (Board Certified Psychiatrists) and was approved for continued unescorted ground privileges.

Curry remained in the "Family Care" program, apparently residing in at least one other Queens home since Dr. Finger provided an update on her condition. Curry told the interviewers she was living in a "Family Care" residence in Queens when she fell and injured her left leg (which prompted her admission to the long-term nursing home where she once lived)".

At the end of a recent visit, a Hillside Manor attendant approached Curry to let her know that lunch would soon be served. When a reporter asked how she like the food at the home, Curry remarked that she does not eat much, since she watches her weight. When told that was not often a concern of someone pushing 100, Curry offered her visitor a broad smile.

As she began navigating toward the dining room, first by pulling herself along via a handrail on the wall, curry accepted an offer of a push. But as the dining room neared, she began using her right leg to propel the creaky wheelchair forward.

"I've got it from here," Curry said as she headed off along down the hallway.

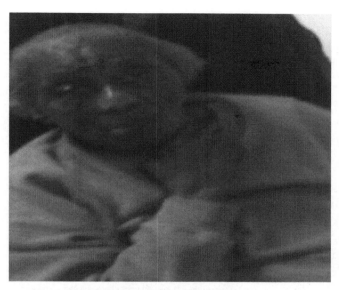

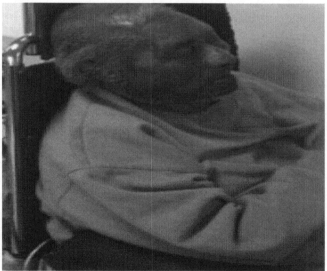

Figure 56: Izola Ware Curry December 2014 - Credited The Smoking Gun

*This chapter is courtesy of The Smoking Gun Report completed 2014
http://www.thesmokinggun.com/documents/crime/the-woman-who-nearly-murdered-martin-luther-king-jr-687453

12 HARLEM HEROS

BLACK AND WHITE HAS NO COLOR

Al Howard and Phil Roman were the two officers that were called on the scene of Blumstein's. They had about thirty minutes left before their shift was to be over. They were heading back to the 28 precinct after responding to a false call of Armed Robbery. Driving down 8th avenue, a call comes in for "Disorderly people in front of Blumstein's Department Store." Phil remembers looking over at Al and looking down at his watch and says, "You know we are really off duty, but let us take a look at this one." "I'll never forget Al turns and looks over to me and says, "Let's do this one for the people"" Phil recants. Technically they were off duty.

Phil remembers seeing the people around King very shocked. He goes on to tell us that there was a lady whom wanted to help and went to pull the letter opener out of his chest but Officer Romano quickly grabbed her hand and twisted it to prevent her from taking the knife out. Romano grew up in the Butcher business and also shares that he had been stabbed a few times, one near the exact location where Dr. King's letter opener was. He said by the looks of where the tter opener was, he could tell it was by or near a main artery and the knife was keeping him alive because Dr. King's shirt was still all white with no blood.

Phil recants thinking that this may have been a set-up and there could have very well been someone still inside Blumstein's that would try to finish the job. This led them to taking extreme precaution. Officer Howard was clear that there would be no way they could go out the front door, as the mob of people was only growing. The only way they could get Dr. King out safely was to create a diversion.

There were two entry and exit points at Blumstein's Department Store. They had the main entrance on 125th street, and a service entry on 124th street (the back entrance) for employees and staff. The mob of concerned citizens was growing rapidly at the front entrance. Officer Howard quickly decided

that he would go to the front of Blumstein's and tell the mob of people that they were going to bring Dr. King through the front. He created the illusion that they needed a walkway so the ambulance could come and wheel Dr. King out the front and into the ambulance. The citizens quickly complied with the hopes that they would have the opportunity to see Dr. King's injury and possibly shake his hand, as this is what they were told. Officer Howard then went back inside and called dispatch (CU) instructing them to send two (2) ambulances. One to the front and one to the back. *recalls*

While officer Howard was addressing the concerned citizens in front of Blumsteins, Officer Romano and two others begin to carry Dr. King in his chair to the back entrance where they had some steps they had to go down. Phil Romano recants how one of the gentlemen helping in carrying Dr. King trips on of the stairs and Dr. King was at the point of rolling over. He quickly and instinctly reacted putting his hand on him to balance him and keep him steady. He remembers that moment as if it were just yesterday because his heart was ready to explode. He says that they never would have believed that is was an accident had Dr. King fallen from his chair and possibly died. Phil Romano remembers that because he was a white officer they would have

109

blamed him and had it be a white black issue which wasn't the case. Finally an ambulance comes around and they place Dr. King inside and off he goes to Harlem Hospital

THE FAB FIVE: SURGICAL TEAM

Despite the two officers efforts, King wasn't saved yet. It was now up to the staff at Harlem Hospital to operate on Dr. King and remove the letter opener from his chest.

The head of surgery at Harlem Hospital was a doctor by the name of Aubre Maynard. However, when Dr. King was brought into the surgical wing, Dr. Maynard was nowhere to be found. So, in Dr. Maynard's place, Doctors John W.V. Cordice and Emil Naclerio were called in to take charge of Dr. King's Surgery. While Dr. Naclerio and Dr. Cordice waited for Dr. Maynard to arrive, they prepared for Dr. King's surgery.

After seeing that King's vital signs were stable, Naclerio and Cordice decided to wait for Dr. Maynard to arrive before moving forward with the surgery. At this point in Maynard's career, he was more of an administrator than practicing surgeon. It was well known amongst the hospital staff that Maynard had long ago abandoned coming in for emergency procedures. Since both Naclerio and Cordice were renowned Thoracic surgeons, they would execute the operation themselves but would allow Maynard to remove the letter opener from King's chest, in what would amount to a ceremonial gesture towards the chairmen of their department. However, Dr. Aubre Maynard had other plans for asserting his name into the history books.

Over an hour after Naclerio and Cordice had prepped King for surgery, Maynard was still nowhere to be found. This entire time he had been only a few miles away at the Plaza Theater on 59th street, watching the new Brigitte Bardor sex comedy, La Parisienne.

Finally arriving at the hospital, Maynard was immediately bombarded by a steaming mad Governor Harriman, who reprimanded the Doctor for being absent for so long. Upon being debriefed by Cordice and Naclerio on King's situation, Maynard went out and talked with the media, immediately positioning himself as the newfound authority on all things King.

While Maynard talked with the media and other visiting surgeons outside, an anesthetic nurse administered the anesthesia, and Cordice and Naclerio began the surgery. They started by making a curving intercostal-chondral incision. This left a cross-shaped scar that king would later joke about throughout his life. They then inserted a rib spreader between the 3rd and 4th intercostal space and got their first glimpse of King's wound. *King told the docs,*

Just as they had suspected, the tip of the blade was resting right on the crotch of his aorta. What would go on to be King's famous line about the experience was indeed true... had Martin Luther King Jr. sneezed, he would've drowned in his own blood.

The first part of the surgery only took about 10 minutes. It was now time for the letter opener to be removed from King's chest. As previously planned, Cordice and Naclerio gifted the opportunity to Dr. Maynard as a goodwill gesture to the chairman of their department. However, when Maynard went to remove the letter opener, he ripped his glove on the side of the blade. As he put on new gloves, Dr. Cordice attached a Kocher clamp to the handle of the letter opener for Maynard to gain more leverage. Naclerio and Cordice grew concerned when Maynard disregarded the clamp and once again tried to remove the letter opener with his hands.

Although either doctor could have easily executed the procedure themselves, it would take two more Kocher clamps and quite a bit of nervous posturing from Cordice and Naclerio before Maynard finally lifted the letter opener out of King's chest.

After removing the letter opener, Maynard left the surgical suite, leaving it to Cordice and Naclerio to finish closing Dr. King's chest. While they did this, Maynard victoriously addressed the media and immediately began to take liberties with the medical details of Dr. King's surgery.

Beyond taking credit for the entire surgery, Dr. Maynard would go on to fabricate other aspects of the procedure. He claimed to reporters that parts of King's rib and sternum had been removed. He would also deny pulling out the blade, asserting that he had instead "pushed up from below". Another falsehood he told reporters was that a hammer and chisel were used to chip off pieces of King's sternum so they could better access the letter opener. While none of these statements were in fact true, Maynard's false testimony would go on to become public record, undeservedly positioning him as a vital part of American History.

In recent years, citizens who were there that fateful day have begun to set the record straight and rightfully position Dr.'s Naclerio and Cordice as the true heroes of the surgery.

Even though the surgery had been successful, Dr. Naclerio still used extreme precaution and care regarding Dr. King's post opt treatment. Doctors assured Dr. King's wife that despite his delicate state and touch and go surgery, he was recovering well and they also described his mental state as, "excellent." They said that Dr. King was in good spirits feeling little pain and required mild sedation.

Dr. King and Mrs. King thanked the surgeons and hospital for their exemplary care in a joint statement. Amazingly, Dr. King felt no ill will towards Izola Ware Curry. Only compassion and concern. They understood that Izola was emotionally disturbed and did not hold her accountable for her actions.

In a press conference held in his hospital room 10 days after the surgery, Dr. King released a statement to the media to discuss his successful surgery.

"I am sorry that I have not been able to accommodate the many newsmen who have expressed a desire to have some word with me earlier." " First let me say that I feel no ill will towards Mrs. Izola Curry and know that thoughtful people do what is in their power to see that she gets the help that she apparently needs if she is to become a free and constructive member of society."

"To Dr. Aubre Maynard, his associates and the splendid hospital staff, I am unable to say enough in expressing my gratitude. To the Governor of New York State, Mr. Averell Harriman, and the many other organizational representatives, I want to offer special thanks. I also want to express my heartfelt appreciation to the thousands of people of all faiths and races, in all walks of life, who have been indicated by telegrams, letters, calls, cards, flowers and other gift their warm concern for my wellbeing. These messages were a great source of strength and support because I know they were a token of respect for the cause we all cherish – freedom and equality for all men."

"The pathetic aspect of this experience is not the injury to one individual. It demonstrates that a climate of hatred and bitterness so permeates areas of our nation that enviably deeds of extreme violence must erupt. Today, it is I. Tomorrow it could be another leader or any man, woman or child who will be the victim of lawlessness and brutality."

"I hope that this experience proves to be socially constructive by demonstrating the urgent necessity for non-violence to govern the affairs of men. Through these days, I have been increasingly able to understand more deeply the hard blows and tragic suffering so many of my people and other members of minority groups experience– all too often, and without cause or reason. The experience of these last few days has deepened my faith in the reverence of the spirit of non-violence, if necessary social change is peacefully to take place. Through experience, I have now come to see more clearly the redemptive power of non-violence."

"I have been brought to see its side of social significance. I am now convinced that if the Negro holds fast to the spirit of non-violence, our struggle and example will challenge and help redeem, not only America but the world."

"Finally, although my thoughts have never left the freedom struggle, I am intensely impatient to rejoin my friends and colleagues to continue the work that we all know must be done regardless of the cost."

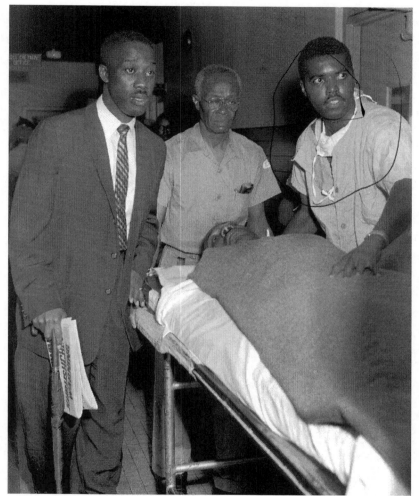

Figure 57: Dr. King on hospital Bed going into Surgery with Dr. Cordice – Credit Associated Press

Figure 58: Dr. King on hospital bed waiting for Surgery

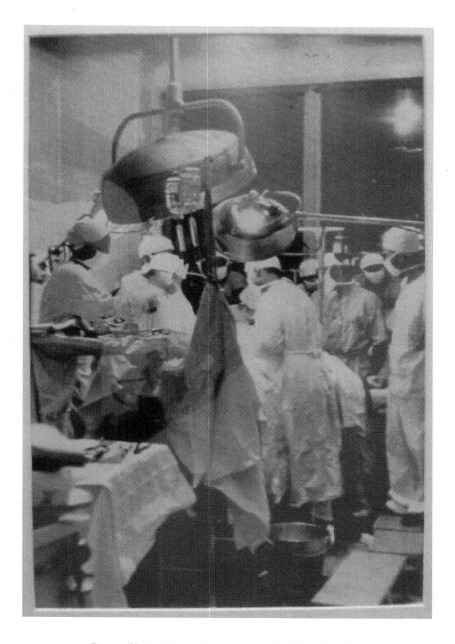

Figure 59: Dr. King in Surgery – credits Vernoll Coleman

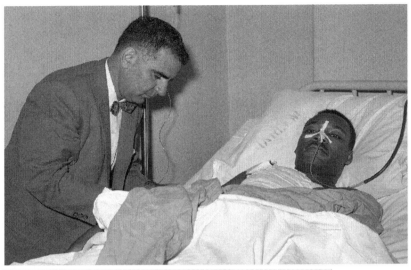

Figure 60: Dr. Naclerio after King's surgery - credit Ron Naclerio and family

Martin Luther King, Jr.
Dexter Avenue Baptist Church
454 Dexter Avenue
Montgomery 4, Alabama

January 6, 1959

Dear Dr. Naclerio:

Ever since leaving New York I have been intending to write you at least a note to express my great appreciation to you for all that you did to preserve my life. Your skilled surgery, coupled with your genuine concern for me as a patient, combined to bring me from a very low ebb in my life to blooming health again. Please know that I will remember your gestures of goodwill so long as the cords of memory shall lengthen.

I hope you have received our gift by now. It is simply a little way to express our gratitude to you for all that you did to ease the load of a difficult period in our lives.

With best wishes to you and yours for health and happiness in 1959. I am

Sincerely yours,

Martin Luther King, Jr.

Dr. Emil Naclerio
35 East 35th Street
New York 16, New York

MLK:mlb

Figure 61: Copy of original letter Dr. King sent Dr. Emil Naclerio after his surgery - Credit Ron Naclerio and Family

Figure 62: Original article of people involved in Dr. King's surviving that fateful day 9.20.1958 - Credit New York Times

13 HALL OF FAME

Isaac Newton, most famous mathematician of the 17th Century was responsible for many scientific discoveries we take for granted today such as the "corrected" Gregorian calendar date. Newton's greatest mathematical discovery was the gravitational relationship between the earth and the moon, and of centrifugal force. Newton was well educated, had access to the best knowledge of his day and was wealthy in later life. He suffered from several "nervous breakdowns" in his life and was known for great fits of rage towards anyone who disagreed with him which some have labeled Bipolar Disorder which was unknown at the time. In 1705 Newton was the first Scientist to be knighted by Queen Anne for his great scientific contributions.

Ludwig can Beethoven, composer, had bipolar disorder which some have said gave him such a creative power that his compositions broke the mold for classical music forever. He was a child prodigy which his father tried to exploit. His "manic" episodes seemed to fuel his creativity. He wrote his most famous works during times of torment, loneliness, and suffering psychotic delusions. It took him 12 years to finish his last and 8th Symphony in total deafness. He then medicated himself with the only drugs available in that day to bring some relief – opium and alcohol – and died several years later of liver disease.

Abraham Lincoln, 16th President of U.S. suffered from severe and debilitating and on occasion suicidal depressions, as recorded by Carl Sandburg in his comprehensive six-volume biographical analysis of his life. "A tendency to melancholy"

Lincoln once wrote in a letter to a friends, "...let it be observed, is a misfortune, not a fault." The most amazing part of his story was the sheer determination with which he willed himself to overcome his serious affliction and still achieve all he was able to achieve for our young and troubled nation at war with itself.

Winston Churchill, Prime Minister of Great Britain who, as one of the "Big Three" (Churchill, Roosevelt and Stalin) to lead the world to the defeat of Hitler in WWII, told in his own writings of suffering from :black dog" Churchill's term for severe and serious depression. Less often talked about are his writings of how he often self-medicated with alcohol to deal with these times. Like so many other famous people with mental illness, he was able to make the great contribution he did through sheer personal determination. There was a nation, he said, and a world depending on his efforts to lead Britain and the world in the defeat of their common and formidable enemy of Nazism.

Virginia Woolf, the British novelist, born of privilege, experienced the mood swings of bipolar disorder her entire life. She wrote to make sense out of her mental chaos and gain control of madness; and was greatly admired for her creative insight into human nature. She was tolerated by friends and family, receiving great care and understanding during her entire life and because of this, never had to face institutionalization, the only medical treatment in those days. She died at her own hand by filling her pockets with stones and walking into a nearby river. The cause of death was determined as "Suicide, while the balance of her mind was disturbed."

Jane Pauley, NBC news broadcaster, since the age of 25, talks candidly about her depression and bipolar illness. In her new book, "Skywriting: A Life Out of the Blue." She tells about her childhood and family problems, and how she discovered her need for medication to control mood swings.

Linda Hamilton, actress, has gone public with her diagnosis of bi-polar disorder diagnosed at a young age. Hamilton, well known for her part with Arnold Schwarzenegger in "The Terminator" movies explains how helpful medication has been for her and the she understands she will have to be on medication for the rest of her life.

Shawn Colvin, Winner of two Grammys in music, talked about her struggle with depression. Colvin has suffered from major depressive disorder for more than 20 years. "During the worst times, I shut the world out, refusing to get out of bed. Even the smallest tasks were overwhelming," she said.

Judy Collins, singer and songwriter, has written a book titled "Sanity and Grace: A Journey of Suicide, Survival and Strength," (2003). The book chronicles her journey as a survivor of depression after the suicide of her 33-year-old son in 1992. She states that her own spiritual life and practice have been a strength for her as she battles with her illness.

Dr. Kay Redfield Jamison, professor of psychiatry at John Hopkins University, Baltimore, MD, author of many books on mental illness. Dr. Jamison has bipolar illness herself and has attempted suicide. Her book "Touched With Fire," lists and describes many famous persons whose lives have been changed by bipolar illness.

Maurice Bernard, portraying Sonny Corinthos on "General Hospital" weekdays on ABC, tells the National Mental Health Association that he suffered from bi-polar disorder for many years before he was diagnosed and given medication to bring his illness under control.

William Styron, author, writes about his own depression in his book, "Darkness Visible: A Memoir of Madness," (1990) and his decision to seek help. His earlier works which he wrote prior to his diagnosis and admission of his illness described with uncanny accuracy, the symptoms and the problems he would experience later in his life. He was one of the first to write about other famous persons who struggled with mental illness and for explaining the almost unexplainable experience of a brain disorder to those who had never experienced it in a way which gained their sympathy and admiration.

John Nash, Noble Prize Winner in mathematics, has faced a lifelong battle with schizophrenia. He was known as the "Phantom of Fine Hall" at Princeton where his reclusive, ghost like figure could be seen roaming around, leaving messages of his mathematical genius on the boards of empty classrooms. His struggle was well documented in the book "A Beautiful Mind," by Sylvia Nasar which was later made into a movie by the same name.

Carrie Fisher, the child of two Hollywood stars (Debbie Reynolds and Eddie Fisher) and actress, in her own right, played Princess Leia in "Star Wars" movies. Early in the 70's she says she started using cocaine. Her experiences with drug addiction led to her first best-selling book, _Postcards from the Edge_. The book was made into a film in 1990 starring Meryl Streep. Her illness comes from her mother's side of the family.

Lionel Aldridge, a football player for the Green Bay Packers during the 1960's, developed paranoid schizophrenia and was homeless for 2 ½ years. "Once I accepted and cooperated with the treatment, I started to beat the illness." He states that he is completely symptom free and that helping others understand mental illness is "therapy" for him.

Eugene O'Neil, famous playwright, author of "Long Day's Journey into Night," and "Ah Wilderness!" came from a deeply troubled family background, suffering from clinical depression the greater portion of his life. His most famous plays were written between 1935 and 1943 despite persistent mental illness. He is the only American playwright to have won the Nobel Prize for literature.

Vivien Leigh, actress made famous by her leading role in "Gone With The Wind" and her creative genius for stage and screen, suffered from serious bouts of manic depression, tuberculosis, and poor health her entire life. It was, in fact, because of her illness, that she was frequently cast into roles that required a personal experience of the torment that comes from the experience of this disease. Vivien was once able to make a full recovery after shock treatments, only to succumb some year later. A nervous breakdown associated with a miscarriage proved to be the unraveling of her marriage with actor Lawrence Olivier who continued to be a devoted friend. She was finally diagnosed with cyclical manic-depression with hallucinations and had to be confined to a nursing home only to recover and return to the screen for her last move. Leigh finally succumbed to the tuberculosis at the young age of 53 while filming "The Ship of Fools". She became known and admired for her ability to fulfill her passionate dream for stardom despite her TB and debilitating manic-depression.

Ruth Graham (daughter of Ruth and Billy Graham) writes about her many years of suffering with depression, drugs, eating disorders and thoughts of suicide in her 2004 book "In every Pew Sits A Broken Heart," Church was never the comfort for her that is seemed to be for others. An adult with a tragic life behind her, she was finally able to talk about it. Being the daughter of a famous preacher she felt she should not have problems. Through the steady love of her family she was able to feel God's forgiveness. Her message today is that being a Christian doesn't guarantee us a perfect life. She hopes her story will give those who want to serve others a place in knowing what to do and say.

Brook Shields talked about her disabling Post-Partum

Depression in her newly published book "Down Came the Rain: My Journey Through Postpartum Depression." Shields reported she first had difficulty bonding with her baby and later thought of hurting it and even killing herself. She was able to gain a significant improvement in her mood through medication and the help of a skilled nurse-helper who recognized her problem and encouraged her to get help.

Chrissy Teigan opened up about the myriad ways PPD took a toll on her mental and physical health. "It's such a major part of my life and so, so many other women's lives," Teigan wrote about the common condition, which affects up to one in seven women in the US. "I'm speaking up now because I want people to know it can happen to anybody and I don't want people who have it to feel embarrassed or to feel alone."

Dwayne "The Rock" Johnson experienced his first of three depressions after sustaining several serious injuries his freshman year of college. "I didn't know what it was," he revealed in an interview with The Hollywood Reporter in 2014. "I didn't know why I didn't want to do anything. I had never experienced anything like that." Johnson later shared what helped him cope. "I found that, with depression, one of the most important things you could realize is that you're not alone," The actor said in an episode of Oprah's Master Class in 2015. "You're not the first to go through it. You're not going to be the last to go through it... I wish I had someone at that time who could just pull me aside and say, 'Hey, it's going to be OK. It will be ok.'"

Demi Lovato has been open about her battles with bipolar disorder, bulimia and addiction. She has been an outspoken advocate for mental health awareness. "It's very important we create conversations, we take away the stigma, and that we stand up for ourselves if we're dealing with the symptoms of a mental illness," Lovato told Variety in 2017. The singer, now five years sober, continued: "It is possible to live well and thrive with a mental illness."

Lisa Nicole Carson opened up about her battle with bipolar disorder in 2015, which sidelined her career for over a decade. "I see a psychiatrist and a psychologist regularly and now just take anti-anxiety medication," she revealed to Essence upon returning to acting in 2015. "I'm tackling the myth that African-American women have to be pillars of strength. We have the right to fall. We have the right not to always have our s--- together."

Kendrick Lamar got candid about his mental health battle in 2015. The Grammy Award- winning artist revealed his struggles with depression and suicidal thoughts in his album "To Pimp a Butterfly." Kendrick raps about the survivor's guilt he feels for leaving his hometown of Compton, California where many of his friends and family still remain.

Gabourey Sidibe talks candidly about mental health in her memoir, "This Is Just My Face: Try Not to Stare." In the book, the actress reveals how she struggled with depression in college and eventually developed bulimia. After experiencing suicidal thoughts, the Oscar nominee turned to a professional for help. "I just accepted depression as something that's part of my anatomy," Sidibe told People in May of 2017. "It's part of my chemistry, it's part of my biology." She continued: "When it's too big for me to just turn around on my own, I see a therapist."

Jon Hamm, who has struggled with addiction and chronic depression, opened up about the benefits of therapy in June of 2018. In an interview with InStyle, the "Mad Men" actor talked about the importance of asking for help when you need it: "Medical attention is medical attention whether it's for your elbow or for your teeth or for your brain. We live in a world where to admit anything negative about yourself is seen as weakness, when it's actually strength. It's not a weak move to say, 'I need help.' In the long run, it's way better, because you have to fix it." Hamm, who completed a 30-day program for alcohol abuse in 2015, has also talked about the benefits of therapy and antidepressants in his battle with chronic depression.

Kid Cudi got candid about his mental health struggles via Facebook in 2016. In a heartfelt message to his fans, the rapper revealed the he has checked himself into rehab for "depression and suicidal urges." "I'm tired of being held back in my life," the rapper wrote. "I deserve to have peace. I deserve to be happy and smiling." Kid Cudi's honest post was met with widespread support. It also spawned a hashtag on Twitter, #YouGoodMan, for black men to open up about their experiences with mental illness and for people to discuss the intersection of race, masculinity, and mental health.

Kristen Bell, who struggles with depression and anxiety, is an outspoken advocate for mental health. In an essay for Motto, the actress slammed the stereotype that people who suffer from mental illnesses are weak. "Anxiety and depression are impervious to accolades or achievements," Bell wrote. "Anyone can be affected, despite their level of success or their place on the food chain." Bell also emphasized the importance of "mental health check-ins: and awareness: "It's important for me to be candid about this so people in similar situations can realize that they are not worthless and that they do have something to offer. We all do."

Additional famous people known to have coped with symptoms of mental illness:

Leo Tolstoy, author
Charles Dickens, English author
John Keats, poet
Michelangelo, artist

Bette Midler, entertainer
Charles Schultz, cartoonist
Dick Clark, entertainer
Irving Berlin, composer
Rosemary Clooney, singer
Jimmy Piersall, Red Sox baseball player
Burgess Meredith, actor
Peter Illyich Tchaikovsky, composer
Charlie Pride, singer
Sylvia Plath, poet and novelist
Janet Jackson, singer
Patty Duke, actress
Roseanne Barr, comedian
Marlon Brando, actor
Maurice Bernard, actor
Buzz Aldrin, astronaut
Margot Kidder, actress
Jonathon Winters, comedian
Pat Conroy, author
Ernest Hemingway, Pulitzer prize winning novelist
Tennessee Williams, American playwright.

14 THE MENTAL STATE OF AMERICA IN 2019

Over 60 million Americans are thought to experience mental illness in a given year, and the impacts of mental illness are undoubtedly felt by millions more in the form of family members, friends, and coworkers. Despite the availability of effective evidence based treatment, about 40% of individuals with serious mental illness do not receive care and many who begin an intervention fail to complete it.

Whether we have a mental illness, know someone who has experienced such a problem, or neither, we need to care about the issue of mental health. After all, we all have mental health. We may not think much about our mental health or even use that phrase, but it's a common element in all our lives. Some people define it as a "state of mind." Others view it as "being content with life" or "feeling good about yourself."

Mental Health is perhaps best explained as how well we cope with daily life and the challenges it brings. When our mental health is good, we can deal better with what comes our way – at home, at work, and just in life. When our mental health is poor, it ca be difficult to function in our daily lives. It is a fluid state with disability and untreated illness at one end, and recovery and complete wellness at the other end. Most of us live and move within the middle range of the spectrum.

A new report, published in Psychological Science in the

Public Interest, a journal of the Association for Psychological Science, investigates stigma as a significant barrier to care for many individuals with mental illness. While stigma is one of many factors that may influence care seeking, it is one that has profound effects for those who suffer from mental illness. Public stigma emerges when pervasive stereotypes – that people with mental illness are dangerous or unpredictable, for example – lead to prejudice against those who suffer from it. The desire to avoid public stigma causes individuals to drop out of treatment or avoid it entirely for fear of being associated with negative stereotypes. Public stigma may also influence the beliefs and behaviors of those closest to individuals with mental illness, including family, friends and care providers.

Mental Health includes our emotional, psychological, and social well-being. It affects how we think, feel, and act. It also helps determine how we handle stress, relate to others, and make choices. Mental Health is important at every stage of life, from childhood and adolescence through adulthood.

A mental illness is a physical illness of the brain that causes disturbances in thinking, behavior, energy or emotion that make it difficult to cope with the ordinary demands of life. Research is starting to uncover the complicated causes of these diseases which can include genetics, brain chemistry, brain structure and/or having another medical condition, like heart disease.

As of 2018, the two most common mental health conditions were :

Anxiety Disorders – More than 18% of adults each year struggle with some type of anxiety disorder, including post traumatic stress disorder (PTSD), obsessive-compulsive disorder and specific phobias.

Mood Disorders – Mood disorders, such as depression and bipolar depression, affect nearly 10% of adults each year and are characterized by difficulties in regulating one's mood.

Although the general perception of mental illness has improved over the past decades, studies show that stigma against mental illness is still powerful, largely due to media stereotypes and lack of education, and that people tend to attach negative stigmas to mental health conditions at a far higher rate than to other diseases and disabilities such as cancer, diabetes or heart disease.

CHILDREN AND ADOLESCENTS

Like adults, children and adolescents can have mental health disorders that interfere with the way they think, feel and act. When untreated, mental health disorders can lead to school failure, family conflicts, drug abuse, violence and even suicide. Untreated mental health disorders are often very costly to families, communities and the health care systems.

Studies show that at least 1 in 5 children and adolescents have a mental health disorder at any given time. Yet, fewer than one in five of these children receive the mental health services they need. Among young people, at least 1 in every 10 has a serious emotional disturbance at any given time.

NAMI

The National Alliance of Mental Illness, is the nation's largest grassroots mental health organization dedicated to building better lives for the millions of Americans affected by mental illness.

PREVALANCE OF MENTAL ILLNESS

- Approximately 1 in 5 adults in the U.S. -43.8 million, or 18.5% experiences mental illness in a given year
- Approximately 1 in 25 adults in the U.S. – 9.8 million, or 4.0% experiences a serious mental illness in a given year that substantially interferes with or limits one or more majors life activities.
- Approximately 1 in 5 youth aged 13-18 (21.4%) experiences a severe mental disorder at some point during their life. For children aged 8-15, the estimate is 13%.
- 1.1% of adults in the U.S. Live with schizophrenia.
- 2.6% of adults in the U.S. live with bipolar disorder
- 6.9% of adults in the U.S. – 16 million – had at least one major depressive episode in the past year.
- 18.1% of adults in the U.S. experienced an anxiety disorder such as posttraumatic stress disorder, obsessive-compulsive disorder and specific phobias.
- Among the 20.2 million adults in the U.S. who experienced a substance use disorder, 50.5% - 10.2 million adults had a co-occurring mental illness.

SOCIAL STATS

- An estimated 26% of homeless adults staying in shelters live with serious mental illness and an estimated 46% live with severe mental illness and/or substance use disorders.
- Approximately 20% of state prisoners and 21% of local jail prisoners have "a recent history" of a mental health condition.
- 70% of youth in juvenile justice systems have at least one mental health condition and at least 20% live with a serious mental illness.
- Only 41% of adults in the U.S. with a mental health condition received mental health services in the past year. Among adults with a serious mental illness, 62.9% received mental health services in the past year.
- Just over half (50.6%) of children with a mental health condition aged 8-15 received mental health services in the previous year.
- African Americans and Hispanic Americans each use mental health services at about one-half the rate of Caucasian Americans and Asian Americans at about one-third the rate.
- Half of all chronic mental illness begins by age 14; three-quarters by age 24. Despite effective treatment, there are long delays, sometimes decades, between the first appearance of symptoms and when people get help.

CONSEQUENCES OF LACK OF TREATMENT

-   Serious mental illness costs America 193.2 billion in lost earnings per year.
-   Mood disorders, including major depression, dysthymic disorder and bipolar disorder, are the third most common cause of hospitalization in the U.S. for both youth and adults aged 18-44.
-   Individuals living with serious mental illness face an increased risk of having chronic medical conditions. Adults in the U.S. living with serious mental illness die on average 25 years earlier than others, largely due to treatable medical conditions.
-   Over one-third (37%) of students with a mental health condition age 14-21 and older who are served by special education drop out – the highest dropout rate of any disability group.
-   Suicide is the 10th leading cause of death in the U.S., and the 2nd leading cause of death for people aged 10-34.
-   More than 90% of people who die by suicide show symptoms of a mental health condition.
-   Each day an estimated 18-22 veterans die by suicide. *www.nami.org/learn-more/mental-health-by-the-numbers*

MENTAL HEALTH AMERICA, INC.

MAHI is committed to promoting mental health as a critical part of overall wellness. They advocate for prevention services for all, early identification and intervention for those at risk, integrated services, care and treatment for those who need it, and recovery as the goal.

They believe that gathering and providing up-to-date data

and information about disparities faced by individuals with mental health problems is a tool for change.

Key Findings:

- Over 44 million American adults have a mental health condition. Since the release of the first State of Mental Health in America report (2015), there has only been a slight decrease in the number of adults who have a mental health condition (from 18.19% to 18.07%)
- Rate of youth experience a mental health condition continues to rise. The rate of youth with Major Depressive Episode (MDE) increased from 11.93% to 12.63%. There was only a 1.5% decrease in the rate of youth with MDE who did receive treatment. Data showed that 62% for youth with MDE received no treatment.
- More Americans are insured and accessing care. We can continue to see the effects of healthcare reform on the rate of adults who are uninsured. This year was a 2.5% reduction in the number of adults with a mental health condition who were uninsured.
- But many Americans experience a mental health condition still report having an unmet need. 1 in 5, or 9 million adults reported having an unmet need.
- Mental health workforce shortage remains. Many states saw some improvement in their individual to mental health provider ratio. But in states with the lowest workforce there was almost 4 times the number individuals to only 1 mental health provider.

Since the release of MHA's first State of Mental Health in America report four years ago, we have seen:

ENCOURAGING DECREASES
in the amount of American adults who have mental health and substance use problems.

ALARMING INCREASES
in adult suicidal ideation and major depressive episodes in youth.

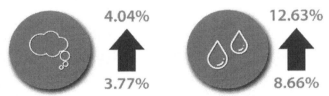

Since the release of last year's State of Mental Health in America report:

The difference between youth experiencing a major depressive episode is becoming more pronounced between the highest and lowest ranked states.

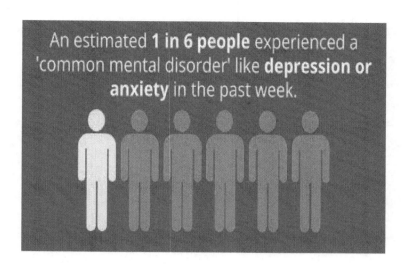

An estimated **1 in 6 people** experienced a 'common mental disorder' like **depression or anxiety** in the past week.

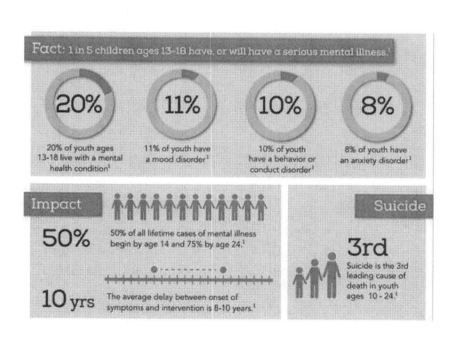

Fact: 1 in 5 children ages 13–18 have, or will have a serious mental illness.[1]

20%
20% of youth ages 13-18 live with a mental health condition[1]

11%
11% of youth have a mood disorder[1]

10%
10% of youth have a behavior or conduct disorder[1]

8%
8% of youth have an anxiety disorder[1]

Impact

50%
50% of all lifetime cases of mental illness begin by age 14 and 75% by age 24.[1]

10 yrs
The average delay between onset of symptoms and intervention is 8-10 years.[1]

Suicide

3rd
Suicide is the 3rd leading cause of death in youth ages 10 - 24.[1]

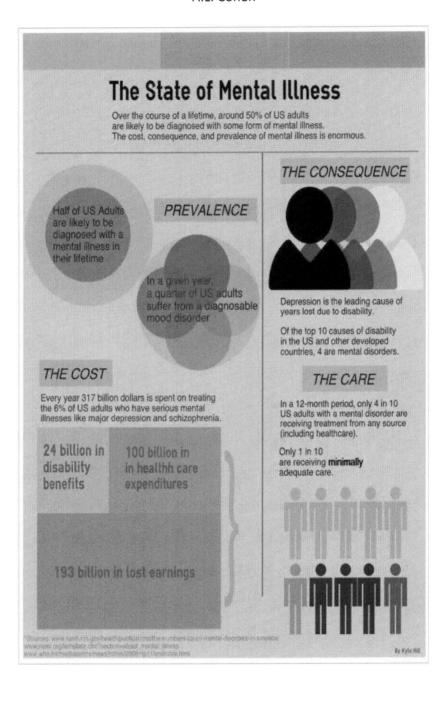

The State of Mental Illness

Over the course of a lifetime, around 50% of US adults
are likely to be diagnosed with some form of mental illness.
The cost, consequence, and prevalence of mental illness is enormous.

PREVALENCE

Half of US Adults are likely to be diagnosed with a mental illness in their lifetime

In a given year, a quarter of US adults suffer from a diagnosable mood disorder

THE CONSEQUENCE

Depression is the leading cause of years lost due to disability.

Of the top 10 causes of disability in the US and other developed countries, 4 are mental disorders.

THE COST

Every year 317 billion dollars is spent on treating the 6% of US adults who have serious mental illnesses like major depression and schizophrenia.

24 billion in disability benefits

100 billion in in healthh care expenditures

193 billion in lost earnings

THE CARE

In a 12-month period, only 4 in 10 US adults with a mental disorder are receiving treatment from any source (including healthcare).

Only 1 in 10 are receiving **minimally** adequate care.

By Kyle Hill

138

15 THE MENTAL STATE OF NEW YORK

THIS REPORT COMES DIRECTLY FROM THE OFFICE OF THE MAYOR, NEW YORK

THE CITY OF NEW YORK
OFFICE OF THE MAYOR
NEW YORK, NY 10007

REPORT: UNDERSTANDING NEW YORK CITY'S MENTAL HEALTH CHALLENGE

While statistics alone cannot capture the devastating human costs of mental illness, they drive home the scope of the mental health crisis facing New York City:

- At least one in five adult New Yorkers is likely to experience a mental health disorder in any given year.

- 8% of NYC public high school students report attempting suicide.

- Consequences of substance misuse are among the leading causes of premature death in every neighborhood in New York City. Each Year, 1,800 deaths and upwards of 70,000 emergency room visits among adults aged 18-64 can be attributed to alcohol use.
- 73,000 New York City public high school students report feeling sad or hopeless each month.

- Approximately 8% of adult New Yorkers experience symptoms of depression each year.

- Major depressive disorder is the single greatest source of disability in NYC. At an given time over half a million adult New Yorkers are estimated to have depression, yet less than 40% report receiving care for it.

- There are $14 billion in estimated annual productivity losses in New York City tied to depression and substance misuse.

- Unintentional drug overdose deaths outnumber both homicide and motor vehicle fatalities.

- The stigma of mental illness has been found to have serious negative effects on hope and an individual's sense of self-esteem. Stigma also increases the severity of psychiatric symptoms and decreases treatment adherence.

Mental illness exacts a devastating social and economic cost on New York and the communities they call home.

Disability Adjusted Life-years

One metric frequently used to describe the impact of mental illness on society relative to other health problems is Disability Adjusted Life-Years (DALYs), which measures the number of years lost to a given disease as a result of loss of life (YLL) or disability (YLD). In other words, DALYs quantify both what makes us feel sick and what kills us. Together, these are often referred to as the "disease burden"

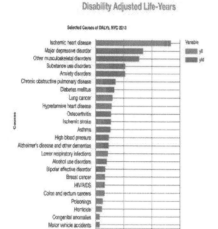

Disability Adjusted Life-Years

Selected Causes of DALYs, NYC 2013

The figure shows that mental illness and substance use disorders are among the leading contributors to the disease burden for New Yorkers, with depressive illness the single largest contributor after heart disease. If the impact of alcohol use disorders and other substance use disorders are added together (they are separated in this figure), they would be the second leading contributor to overall disease burden in New York City.

Disability related to mental illness (YLD) can have significant real-life consequences for New Yorkers. It can lead to job loss, dropping out of school, struggles with parenting, losing one's housing, having difficulty making and keeping friends, and other challenges.

But DALYs only show a part of the impact. They do not capture the wide variety of related health problems that often afflict people with mental illness, and therefore underestimate the full extent of their suffering. A few additional statistics make this clear:

- In the U.S., the average life expectancy of people with a mental illness is approximately eight years less than people without one. Many people with mental illness or substance use disorders experience a substantial gap in the quality of routine medical care, especially when it comes to general medical and cardiovascular care.

- Experiencing a period of mental illness increases a person's likelihood of developing a physical illness, including diabetes, hypertension, and high cholesterol.

- Adults in NYC with Serious Mental Illness (SMI) are three times more likely to smoke, and they are less likely to exercise or eat fruits or vegetables. It is therefore not surprising that they are twice as likely to have two or more chronic medial illnesses when compared to adults without SMI.

- In the U.S. prolonged depression can more than double the risk of stroke in people over 50 years of age.

DALYs also do not capture people who may have a diagnosable mental illness, but who still may suffer from poor mental health. To support the mental well-being of all New Yorkers and move the needle on DALYs, we need to focus on our society itself – which means addressing big issues like racism, income inequality, and disparities in community resources or access to education and opportunity while also providing targeted individual care when needed.

The economic burden of mental illness

Finally, DALYs do not capture the considerable economic burden mental illness and substance misuse exact on society. In New York, mental illness and substance misuse together have a tremendous impact on a variety of social costs, including health

Economic Losses from Mental Health and Substance Use Factors[197]
(NYC-wide annual estimate)

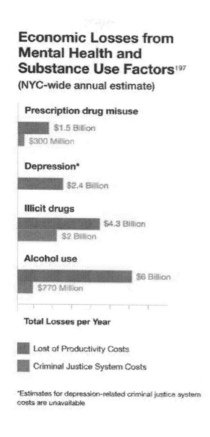

Prescription drug misuse
$1.5 Billion
$300 Million

Depression*
$2.4 Billion

Illicit drugs
$4.3 Billion
$2 Billion

Alcohol use
$6 Billion
$770 Million

Total Losses per Year

■ Lost of Productivity Costs
■ Criminal Justice System Costs

*Estimates for depression-related criminal justice system costs are unavailable

care, criminal justice, and lost productivity.

- Alcohol misuse is estimated to cost NYC nearly $6 billion in citywide economic productivity losses every year, while depression accounts for $2.4 billion in losses.

- Misuse of illicit and prescription drugs and alcohol in NYC together cost approximately $1 billion in criminal justice expenditures annually.

As troubling as these numbers are, they reflect only a fraction of the total costs. Measuring the cost of productivity losses to a business may not fully capture the cost of mental illness in the workplace. In a study in London, for example, estimates of lost earnings for individuals with mental illness were double the estimate of economic losses in productivity. In addition, these figures also do not fully account for costs incurred by caregivers, family members, and the community at large.

It is also important to consider the enormous amount of money we spend on overall health care costs. In 2013, more than 630,000 New Yorkers with health insurance (Medicaid, Medicare or commercial insurance) saw a provider who diagnosed a mental illness. While this group only accounted for

8.3% of the population, the cost of their health care- almost $17 billion – represented approximately 25.6% of total health care expenditures paid by these insurance sources in New York City. This figure does not capture the cost of care for the many New Yorkers who are uninsured.

Risks to mental health affect New Yorkers at every stage in their lives

Mental illness or distress can occur at any point during our lives. But there are certain stages that present greater risks to mental health – and also a greater opportunity to intervene with effective support that could provide the tools to achieve long-term mental wellness.

Early years

The first few years of life play a profound role in a person's ability to manage emotions in a healthy way. Childhood exposure to adverse events – such as domestic violence, neglect, abuse, family financial strain, and divorce (or certain community conditions such as unsafe neighborhoods) – are all associated with chronic diseases and threats to mental health in adulthood.

These circumstances can also contribute to toxic stress, which is the strong, unrelieved activation of the body's stress management system in the absence of protective support. Toxic stress can change the architecture of the developing brain and have a devastating lifelong impact. For example:

- Adolescents exposed to childhood adversity, including family malfunctioning, abuse, neglect, violence, and economic adversity, are nearly twice as likely as their peers to experience the onset of mental disorders, and the risk to their mental health grows with additional exposures.

- Even neighborhood violence that a child does not directly experience, such as a nearby homicide, has been shown to reduce cognitive performance.

- Experiencing two or more adverse events during childhood is associated with a two-to-eight-fold increase in depression, anxiety, and tobacco and marijuana use.

- Early identification of developmental delays and disabilities in young children through timely screening can reduce the risk for depression, anxiety, and overall psychological distress.

Tragically, for too many young New Yorkers are at risk for poor mental health. A 2011-2012 survey found that approximately 18% of children in New York State between the ages of zero and 17 experienced two or more adverse family experiences in their lifetime, which predicts poor mental health and physical health outcomes later in life.

Adolescence

Adolescence is a period when mental health conditions often first emerge, ranging from substance misuse to psychosis.

- In a biennial survey of NYC public high schools, more than one in four students reported feeling persistently sad or hopeless in the past year. This is a common predictor of depressive illness.

- In 2013, one in ten NYC public high school students reported being hit, slapped, or physically hurt by someone they were dating or going out with within the past year.

- A young person who is exposed to pervasive violence has

-   a 50% increased risk of having elevated depressive symptoms and anxiety. Each episode of violence (dating violence, bullying, physical fighting, family violence) is associated with an increased risk of that young person also being a perpetrator of violence by anywhere from 35% to 144%.

-   An estimated 7,000 emergency room visits each year in NYC involve alcohol use among individuals under 21 years of age.

-   8% of NYC public high school students report attempting suicide. That percentage doubles if a student has been bullied on school grounds, which 18% of students experience.

-   Gay and lesbian youth in New York City experience nearly twice as much bullying on school property as heterosexual youth, and are more than twice as likely to attempt suicide. And LGBT youth of color may also experience compounded stressors related to racism and discrimination.

Young adulthood

Young adulthood is a time of continuing development and the creating of lifelong social networks and habits. It is also often a period when mental illnesses emerge, especially mood, psychotic, and substance use disorders. According to national studies, three quarters of all mental health and substance use disorders start by age 24.

Among 1,000 City University of New York undergraduates who responded to a campus survey:

-   19% met criteria for depression

- 26% reported significant anxiety

- Of those who reported depressive symptoms, only 10% received help from their college counseling or health center.

Parenthood

Becoming a parent can be a joyful experience, but it also associated with a number of mental health risks. While this is true for both fathers and mothers, depression in mothers is more common. A mother's depression affects her own mental and physical health, heightens the child's risk of psychiatric illness, lowers the chances of the child developing emotional strength and resilience, and decreases the child's likelihood of receiving optimal health care.

Despite the important effect of parenting on mental health, we have limited data when it comes to identifying individuals or areas of the city where risk is high. Here is what we do know:

- 12% of NYC mothers exhibit symptoms of depression in the months after giving birth.

- It is estimated that as many as 20% of lower-income mothers develop symptoms of depression after pregnancy.

- While a higher risk of depression persists in mothers with young children up to five years of age, more than one-third of mothers in one study had not sought help for their mood.

- Parent caregivers of children with chronic illness, including intellectual/developmental disabilities are at greater risk for depression as well.

- Women younger than 19 years old report experiencing post-partum depression at higher rates than women 20 years old and older.

Acting early with parents also helps us act early for their children. Evidence shows that providing parents with preventive interventions for mental illness reduces the risk of their child developing a mental disorder and psychological symptoms later in life by 40%.

Adulthood

Adult mental illness often builds upon earlier events, but this period of life can present additional threats to mental health such as the loss of a job, economic vulnerability, and divorce. Overall, bipolar illness, schizophrenia, PTSD, OCD, and other anxiety disorders can also exert their greatest impact in adulthood, contributing to disability and social and economic difficulties and challenging families. Family support is a key promoter of resilience, mental health, and connection to quality care for people suffering from these disorders. Employment is another crucial factor for self-sufficiency in adults, and yet individuals experiencing mental illness and intellectual and development disabilities are significantly underrepresented in the workforce.

Adulthood can also be a time of trauma, especially in the form of intimate partner and other violence. Nearly one out of every 50 adult New Yorkers report that they are physically fearful of their partner. And this is an issue that cuts across every demographic – our Family Justice Centers, which serve victims of domestic violence, have worked with clients from every residential zip code in New York City. It is also important to note that abuse isn't always physical. According to a 2011 study by the Centers for Disease Control, "nearly half of all women and men in the United States have experienced psychological aggression by an intimate partner in their lifetime (48.4% for women and 48.8% for men)." The same study found that more than 20% of individuals who suffered intimate partner abuse also suffered from one or more symptoms of Post-Traumatic Stress Syndrome.

Late Adulthood

Our eldest citizens, especially if they are socially isolated or impaired from diminished overall health, have an escalated risk for depression and suicide.

- The incidence of depression is higher among subpopulations of elders compared to the general population, with rates of major depression occurring in 13.5% of elder home health care recipients.

- As mentioned, in some studies roughly one-third of widows and widowers meet the criteria for depression in the first month after the death of their spouse. Half of these individuals – most of whom are senior citizens – remain clinically depressed a year later.

- In the U.S. the suicide rate of older adults (65+) is roughly 50% higher than the general population, with white men over 85 committing suicide at 4 times the rate of the general population.

- Information from the National Household Survey on Drug Use predicted that as baby boomers age, treatment rates for substance use disorders among older adults (50+) may increase by as much as 70%.

- Older parent caregivers of those with intellectual / developmental disabilities may be at a relatively greater risk for psychological stress and other mental health conditions.

- 92 out of every 1,000 older New York City residents were victims of elder abuse in a one year period.

Mental health varies across the city

We all face threats to our mental health. But these threats are distributed unequally, and are especially present in neighborhoods where historic neglect has resulted from racial discrimination and other longstanding structural inequities.

Poverty

In New York City, the distribution of mental illness varies strongly by income:

- SMI is more than twice as common for adults who live below 200% of the federal poverty level (FPL) compared to those living 200% above it.

- In NYC, most of the young children with reported mental health disorders live in poverty. Of all NYC children between the ages o two and five whose parents report their child being diagnosed with at least one of five common mental health disorders, 90% live in poverty.

Race and ethnicity

The prevalence, diagnosis, and treatment of mental illness can vary widely among racial and ethnic groups. For example:

- In New York City, Latina adolescents feel disproportionately sad or hopeless and are more likely to attempt suicide.

- In the United States, African Americans are less likely than whites to be diagnosed with common mental illnesses like depression and anxiety. But when they are diagnosed with a mental illness, African Americans are more likely than whites to experience a persistent and severe illness, this may in part be due to biases in diagnosis. For example, African Americans are more likely to be given a diagnosis of schizophrenia and other psychotic disorders, and that is true even when they have the same symptoms as white people.

This highlights a significant challenge to understanding the prevalence of mental illness in a given population. Provider biases can affect the diagnosis and treatment of mental illness, and the use of mental illness labels can sometimes be driven by social judgments and prejudice. It is therefore uncertain to what degree data on racial, ethnic, or gender differences in mental health data reflect the true presence of illness.

We must also look closely at differences within racial groups. While diagnosis rates for depression and anxiety among adult Latinos in recent years are relatively comparable to whites, there are large variations within Latinos. For example, people of Puerto Rican descent were 54% more likely to have more severe depressive symptoms than people of Mexican descent.

Every New Yorker is shaped by factors such as race, culture, ethnicity, income, and geography in unique and complex ways. Because an individual simultaneously occupies more than one identity, and because of the many social prejudices and obstacles that can accompany each of these identities, a better understanding of how these different experiences and histories shape mental health outcomes – whether as a diagnosable illness, or as other emotional suffering that needs better solutions – is critical to designing effective responses.

Access to care varies throughout the city

Despite the fact that people of color and those in poverty bear the greatest mental health burden they are among the least likely to get help.

- African Americans and Asians are less likely to receive counseling/therapy or take medication for their illness than whites, according to a survey of NYC residents.

- Receipt of mental health treatment has been found to be lower for African Americans and Latino's compared to whites.

- National studies suggest that African Americans can be half as likely as whites to receive community-based mental health care, but as much twice as likely to be hospitalized.

The likelihood of someone have a psychiatric hospitalization in New York City varies dramatically by neighborhood and income.

People from the city's lowest income neighborhoods are twice as likely to be hospitalized for mental illness compared to residents from the highest income neighborhoods.

The reasons behind these variations across our neighborhoods reflect more than a need for hospitalization; they also reflect a lack of other options. High rates of psychiatric hospitalization likely reflect the challenges residents of some neighborhoods face, including difficulty accessing preventive services and early care, greater exposure to stressors such as housing instability, and interruptions in health insurance.

Taking a public health approach to mental illness means examining these root causes. In other words, we cannot limit ourselves to advocating for access to treatment – we must also examine the context that results in certain communities bearing such a disproportionate share of the collective burden.

People are not connected to the right care when they need it

Our mental health treatment system is often criticized as not being a "system" at all, for the simple reason that it doesn't do a good job of reaching people, directing them to effective care, and make sure they actually receive the care they need. 41% of New York City adults with an SMI said they need treatment at some point in the past year but did not receive it or delayed getting it. And when New Yorkers do receive care, it is often inefficient and ineffective.

Consider Medicaid spending in New York City. Medicaid is the source of health insurance for approximately 3 million New Yorkers. In 2014, the overall health costs for people with a mental illness or substance use-related diagnosis were more than three times the cost for people without these diagnoses. Individuals with any mental illness diagnosis or indication of substance misuse experience three times the number of emergency room visits for physical health care issues, and six times the number of medical inpatient hospital days compared to people without those conditions. These overall patterns hold for other sources of insurance as well. And other data suggests that older patients with symptoms of depression have roughly 50% higher overall health care costs than non-depressed seniors.

Although high-cost mental and medical care services clearly fuel each other, they are generally not well-coordinated or well-integrated. This serves to further escalate costs.

It's not just that hospitalization is expensive – it is also ineffective if not followed by regular, ongoing outpatient treatment in the community. Yet in the first six months of 2014, only about one in three people who completed a psychiatric hospitalization in New York City were successfully linked to follow-up outpatient treatment within 30 days of leaving the hospital.

This illustrates a fundamental problem: Despite the substantial resources we invest and spend on mental health, the treatment system falls short on results. A big reason for this failure is the fact that care is often not evidence-based, in two key ways:

- **The treatment often doesn't fit the need.** Too often, we connect people to resources and treatment that do not get to the heart of the problem. For example, a disproportionate share of Medicaid dollars is devoted to families with complex needs that are affected by poverty, abuse, neglect, and mental health challenges. While children in these families who suffer from mental illness may receive treatment or support services, the services typically focus on the child and fail to address the ways in which the mental health of the child is inextricably tied to the larger family dynamic. In other situations, specialized treatment options are often used where lighter touches, such as support groups or self-care, would be more effective instead.

- **Much of the care is not delivered properly.** Examples of this abound:

  o Approximately half of all treatment for major depressive illness in the U.S. does not follow expert-recommended best practices.
  o Almost three-quarters of youth insured by Medicaid who receive antipsychotics were prescribed these drugs "off-label", that is, for conditions not approved by the Food and Drug Administration. While off-label use is common and not illegal, the use of these medications for children in the absence of firm evidence of their efficacy has garnered significant concern and scrutiny.

o A recent national study suggests that increased access to mental health treatment for youth over the last decade may contribute to the overuse of anti-depressant and stimulant medications.

We need more information to be effective

Despite the many data points described here, there remain many questions about where and how mental health threats take root, how to better match what we are doing with where we can make the biggest impact, and the comparative value and quality of treatment and intervention options.

And we especially need to better measure mental health itself through adopting new measures and tools. In order to effectively tailor both our treatment and prevention efforts, we must have a thorough and data-based understanding of how mental illness, substance misuse, and threats to mental health manifest. To move forward and address mental health priorities we should also rethink traditional methods for gathering information about mental health.

Some countries are beginning to measure "well-being" and the position attributes of mental health. Similarly, it would be useful to capture not just neighborhood effects that pose threats to mental health, but also positive attributes that contribute to the resiliency of individuals and communities. Better data about both mental health and mental illness will help us make better decisions and smarter choices.

ABOUT THE AUTHOR

A.L Cohen is the Founder and CEO of Jireh Management Group (JMG). He oversees the company's diverse and valuable portfolio of business development services, media production, publications and strong brand representation across the entertainment industry.

With over 25 years of experience in leadership, Cohen masters the art of strategic thinking and the development of influential relationships. He is an industry leader who understands the benefits of the inclusion of high level public relation solutions, cohesive marketing and broad communication ranges to meet business objectives.

As the founder of JMG, Cohen aims to establish a global, significant and engaging presence within communities by using education as the core resource to bridging the gaps. Cohen has a sharp, cutting-edge mindset that influences behavior, change and motivates action. It is this internal commitment that has outwardly birthed Jireh Management Group Productions, the home of "When Harlem Saved a King", a documentary which tells the story of the 1958 stabbing of Dr. Martin Luther King in Harlem, New York by a demented black woman. A story that brings awareness to a pivotal point in history and highlights mental illness which continues to be a disproportional community disparity.

Cohen is a graduate of the New York Institute of Finance and the Borough of Manhattan Community College, from which he received an associate degree in finance. His certification includes Youth Crisis and Prevention Arbitrator from former New York City Mayor David Dinkins; Lifetime Member, Young Fathers Program of New Jersey; Behavior Modification and Therapeutic Intervention from St. Christopher Otillie; Conflict Resolution and Intergroup Relations from the City of New York.

A.L. Cohen is married to Janet Cohen and has a two beautiful daughters Sabella, 3 and Mila 2 years old.

SOURCES

Any Anxiety Disorder Among Adults. (n.d.) Retrieved January 16, 2016 from http://www.nimh.nih.gov/health/statistics/prevalence/any-anxiety-among-adults.shtml. pp.100

Any Disorder Among Children. (n.d.) Retrieved January 16, 2015, from http://www.nimh.nih.gov/health/statistics/prevalence/any-disorder-among-children.shtml. pp.100

Any Mental Illness (AMI) Among Adults. (n.d.) Retrieved October 23, 2015 from http://www.nimh.nih.gov/health/statistics/prevalence/any-mental-illness-ami-among-adults.shtml. pp.100

Arsenault, Raymond (2006). Freedom Riders: 1961 and the Struggle for Racial Justice. Oxford University Press. ISBN 9781416558682. pp.6

Arroyo, Elizabeth (2006). "Medgar Evers". In Palmer, Colin A. Encyclopedia of African-American Culture and History (2nd ed.). London, England: Macmillan. P. 738. ISBN 978-0028658162. pp.29

Barker, L. and Jones, M. "African Americans and the American Political System." New York: Pearson Press, 1998.

Bipolar Disorder Among Adults. (n.d). Retrieved January 16, 2015, from http://www.nimh.nih.gov/health/statistics/prevalence/bipolar-disorder-among-adults.shtml. pp.100

Colton, C.W. & Manderscheid, R.W. (2006). Congruencies in the Increased Mortality Rates, Years of Potential Life Lost, and Causes of Death Among Public Mental Health Clients in Eight States. *Preventing Chronic Disease: Public Health Research, Practice and Polices*, 3(2), 1-14. pp.101

Daley, Michael (January 20, 2914). "The Black and White Men Who Saved Martin Luther King's Life" retrieved January 2, 2015 from The Daily Beast at http://www.thedailybeast.com/articles/2014/01/19/the-black-and-white-men-who-saved-dr-martin-luther-king-jr. pp.43

Ellis, Kate, Smith, Stephen (2011). "State of Siege: Mississippi Whites and the Civil Rights Movement". American Public Media. Retrieved February 11, 2011. pp.29

Endler, Joseph and Wald, Richard C. (n.d.). Harlem Woman Stab's Rev. Martin Luther King: Negro Leader is Attacked in Store As He Autographs Copies of book. Courtesy U.S. Department of Justice Federal Bureau of Investigation. pp.28

Forman, James (1972). The Making of Black Revolutionaries. University of Washington Press. ISBN 9780295976594. pp.6

Glaze, L.E. & James, D.J. (2006). Mental Health Problems of Prison and Jail Inmates. Bureau of Justice Statistics Special Report. U.S. Department of Justice, Office of Justice Programs Washington, D.C. Retrieved March 5, 2013, from http://bjs.ojp.usdoj.gov/content/pub/pdf/mhppji.pdf. pp.102

Halpern, M. "Moving North: African Americans and the Great Migration 1915-1930." New York: National Geographic Children's Books, 2005.

Hendricks, A. (1958, September 22). King Just Missed Death, Will Need 3 months to recover, MD Says. The New York Post. pp.26

Hughes, C.J., (n.d.). "Hudson Valley Psychiatric Hospitals: Insane Asylums and Psych Centers of Upstate NY", Hudson Valley Magazine, retrieved September 11, 2013. pp.31

Insel, T.R. (2008). Assessing the Economic Costs of Serious Mental Illness. The American Journal of Psychiatry. 165(6), 663-665. Pp.101

Isometsa, E.T., (2001). Psychological Autopsy Studies – A Review. European Psychiatry, 16(7), 379-85. pp.102

Kessler, R.C. et al. (2005). Prevalence, Severity, and Comorbidity of 12 Month DSMIV Disorders in the National Comorbitity Survey Replication. Archives of General Psychiatry, 62(6), 593-602. Retrieved January 16, 2015, from http://archpsyc.jamanetwork.com/article.aspx?articleid=2086 71. pp.101

King, K. "African American Politics." New York: Polity Press, 2007

King, M.L. "Statement from Harlem Hospital." New York, 1958

Lee, H. (1958, September 22) Rev. King Mends; Was a Sneeze Away from Death. Unknown Newspaper Article. pp.83

Levison, Stanley David (n.d.). King Institute Resources. Retrieved May 8, 2017. pp.9

Major Depression Among Adults. (n.d.) Retrieved January 16, 2015, from

http://www.nimh.nih.gov/health/statistics/prevalence/major
-depression-among-adults.shtml. pp.100

Mental Health America of the Heartland (n.d.) Why Mental
Health Matters. Kansas City, MO. Retrieved January 2019 from
http://mhah.org/who-we-are/why-mental-health-matters.
pp.103

Mental Health Ministries (n.d.). Famous people and Mental
Illness. Retrieved January 2019 from
http://mentalhealthministries.net/resources/flyers/famous_p
eople/famouspeople.pdf. pp.99

McDuffie, E.S. "Sojourning for Freedom: Black Women,
American Communism and the Making of the Black left
Feminism." North Carolina: Duke University Press, 2011.
pp.19

MLK, MBU, Martin Luther King Jr., Papers. (1954-1968),
Howard Gotlieb Archival Research Center, Boston University,
Boston MA.

National Alliance of Mental Illness (n.d.). Mental Health By
The Numbers. Retrieved January 1, 2019 from
https://www.nami.org/learn-more/mental-health-by-the-
numbers. pp.102

National Archives (n.d.). Izola Ware Curry articles courtesy of
The National Archives. September 1958 – December 1958
from http://archive.org/stream/IzolaWareCurry/100-HQ-
106679-A_Izola_Curry_djvu.txt. pp.34

National Association of State Mental Health Program
Directors Council. (2006). Morbidity and Mortality in People
with Serious Mental Illness. Alexandria, VA: Parks J. pp.98

National Center for Mental Health and Juvenile Justice. (2007). Blueprint for Change: A Comprehensive Model for the Identification and Treatment of Youth with Mental Health Needs in Contact with the Juvenile Justtice System. Delmar, N.Y: Skowya, K.R. & cocozza, J.J. retrieved January 16, 2015, from http://www.ncmjff.com/wp-content/uploads/2013/07/2007_Blueprint_for_Change_Full_report.pdf. pp.102

National Institutes of Mental Health. (2018). "Suicide". pp.102

National Institute of Mental Health. (September 4, 2014.) Stigma as a Barrier to Mental Health. Grant MH08598 to Patrick W. Corrigan and Grant MG075867 to Benjamin G. Druss. pp.104

Pearl, M. and Savelson, E. (1958, September 21). Woman Stabs Rev. King Here. New York Mirror. pp.68

Pearson, Hughes. "When Harlem Nearly Killed King: The 1958 stabbing of Dr. Martin Luther King, Jr." New York: Seven Stories Press, 2004

Pepper, W.F. "An Act of State: The Execution of Dr. Martin Luther King, Jr." New York: Verson Press, 2008.

Porter, L. "Assassination: A History of Political Murder." New York: Overlook Hardcover, 2010.

Poston, T. (1958, September 22). The Woman Needs Help, Not Jail: King. The New York Post,

Serious Mental Illness (SMI) Among Adults. (n.d.) Retrieved October 23, 2015, from http://www.nimh.nih.gov/health/statistics/prevalence/serious-mental-illness-smi-among-us-adults.shtml. pp.100

Schizophrenia. (n.d) Retrieved January 16, 2015, from http://www.nimh.nih.gov/health/statistics/prevalence/schizo phrenia.shtml. pp.100

Sernett, M.C. "Bound for the Promised Land: African American Religion and the Great Migration (The Eric C. Lincoln Series on the Black Experience) North Carolina: Duke University Press Book, 1997. Pp.19

Substance Abuse and Mental Health Services Administration, Results from the 2014 National Survey on Drug Use and Health: Mental Health Findings, NSDUH Series H-50, HHS Publication No. (SMA) 15-4927. Rockville, MD: Substance Abuse and Mental Health Services Administration. (2015). Retrieved October 27, 2015 from http://www.samhsa.gov/data/sites/default/files/NSDUH-FRR1-2014/NSDUHFRR1-2014.pdf. pp.100

Tyson, Timothy B. (2001). Radio Free Dixie: Robert F. Williams and the Roots of Black Power. University of North Carolina Press. ISBN 9780807849231. pp.16

Tuck, Stephen G.N. (2001). Beyond Atlanta: The Struggle for Racial Equality in Georgia, 1940-1980. University of Georgia Press. ISBN 978082325286. pp.7

U.S. Department of Education. (2014). 35th Annual Report to Congress on the Implementation of the Individuals with Disabilities Education Act, 2013. Washington, DC: U.S. Department of Education. Retrieved January 16, 2015, from http://www2.ed.gov/about/reports/annual/osep/2013/part s-b-c/35th-idea-arc.pdf.

U.S. Department of Housing and Urban Development, Office of Community Planning and Development. (2011). The 2010 annual Homeless Assessment Report to Congress. Retrieved January 16, 2015, from http://www.hudexchange.info/resources/documents/ 2010HomelessAssessment. pp.102

Use of Mental Health Services and Treatment Among Children. (n.d.). Retrieved January 16, 2015, from http://www.nimh.nih.gov/health/statistics/prevalance/use-of-mental-health-services-and-treatment-among-children.shtml. pp102

Unknown Author. (September 23, 1958). Georgians send King's Attacker Cash for Needs. Cartersville, GA. Courtesy of The U.S. Department of Justice, Federal Bureau of Investigation. pp.48

Upchurch, Thomas Adams (2008). Race Relations in the United States, 1960-1980. Westport Connecticut: Greenwood Press. p.14. pp.13

Walsh, R. and Lee, H. (1958, September 21). Woman stabs Negro King Leader. Sunday News. pp.47

Williams, K.E. "They Left Great Marks on Me: African American Testimonies of Racial Violence from Emancipation to WWI." New York: New York University Press, 2012. pp.44

Williams, Reggie (July 2, 2005). "Remembering Medgar". Afro King-American Red Star. p. A1. pp.29

Wikipedia (n.d.). Lewis H. Michaux. Retrieved October 2018 from http://en.wikipedia.org/wiki/Lewis_H.Michaux. pp.9

Yang, Lucy. December 27, 2017. 23 Celebrities who have opened up about their struggles with mental illness. The Insider. Retrieved December 2018 from https://www.thisisinsider.com/celebrities-depression-anxiety-mental-illness. pp.95-97

Yasinac, Rob (n.d.). "Matteawan State Hospital" at Hudson Valley ruins. pp.58

Chapter 15 sources:

---

1 There is surprisingly limited data on which to base very specific descriptions of mental illness in our communities. And as will be discussed in this report, formal definitions of "illness" and information we have about them only capture a part of how threats to mental health, affect so much of our lives. This is one reason why this Roadmap will underscore the need for developing better information gathering methods to support a strong program for mental health. Existing studies indicate that somewhere near the range of 18-26% of adults each year experience a defined mental health disorder—a term which throughout this report is intended to also include substance use disorders— in a given year. (1) The National Comorbidity Survey-Replication (NCS-R) estimates 26%1 of US adults have a mental health disorder in a given year, using a gold-standard survey method that uses a diagnostic checklist and assessed for several disorders including anxiety, mood, impulse control, and substance use disorders. (2) The National Survey on Drug Use and Health (NSDUH) estimates prevalence of mental health disorders based on extrapolating predictions from a similar diagnostic interview. Based on these predictions, approximately 19% of adults in New York State have a mental health disorder in a given year, not including

substance use disorders. (3) Using a similar model, our own NYC data estimates the prevalence of mental health disorders –though excluding substance use disorders— at 21%. Given that (4) the NSDUH estimates 8% of New York State adults have a substance use disorder in a given year, the overall NYC prevalence of mental illness is potentially even higher than 21%. Sources: 1) Kessler RC, Chiu WT; Demler O, Walters EE. Prevalence, Severity, and Comorbidity of 12-Month DSM-IV Disorders in the National Comorbidity Survey Replication, Archives of General Psychiatry, (2005) 62: 617-627; 2) http://www.samhsa.gov/data/sites/default/files/NSDUHsae SpecificStates2013/NSDUHsaeNewYork2013. pdf; 3) Thorpe LE, Greene C, Freeman A, at al. Rationale, design and respondent characteristics of the 2013–2014 New York City Health and Nutrition Examination Survey (NYC HANES 2013–2014). Preventive Medicine Reports, 2015.http://www. samhsa.gov/data/sites/default/files/NSDUHsaeSpecificState s2013/ NSDUHsaeNewYork2013.pdf

2 New York City Department of Health and Mental Hygiene in collaboration with the NYC Department of Education. Youth Risk Behavior Survey 2013: http://www.nyc. gov/html/doh/html/episrv/episrv-youthriskbehavior.shtml

3 Zimmerman R, Li W, Lee E, Lasner-Frater L, Van Wye G, Kelley D, Kennedy J, Maduro G, Sun Y. Summary of Vital Statistics, 2013: Mortality. New York, NY: New York City Department of Health and Mental Hygiene, Office of Vital Statistics, 2015.

4 New York State Department of Health Statewide Planning and Research Cooperative System (SPARCS) Unpublished Raw Data, 2012.

5 New York City Department of Health and Mental Hygiene. New York City Youth Risk Behavior Survey Unpublished Raw Data, 2013.

[6] New York City Department of Health and Mental Hygiene. New York City Health and Nutrition Examination Survey Unpublished Raw Data, 2013.

[7] Muenning, P., Goldsmith, J.A., El-Sayed A.M., Goldmann, E.S., Quan, R., Barracks S., Cheung J., Behavioral Health in New York City: The Burden, Cost, and Return on Investment. Unpublished Raw Data, 2015.

[8] Thorpe LE, Greene C, Freeman A, et al. Rationale, design and respondent characteristics of the 2013–2014 New York City Health and Nutrition Examination Survey (NYC HANES 2013–2014). Preventive Medicine Reports, 2: 580, 2015.

[9] Muenning, P., Goldsmith, J.A., El-Sayed A.M., Goldmann, E.S., Quan, R., Barracks S., Cheung J., Behavioral Health in New York City: TheBurden, Cost, and Return on Investment. Unpublished Raw Data, 2015.

[10] New York City Department of Health and Mental Hygiene. Vital Statistics MortalityData Unpublished Raw Data, 2013.

[11] Livingston J.D., Boyd J.E. Correlates and Consequences of Internalized Stigma for People Living with Mental Illness: A Systematic Review and Meta-analysis. Social Science & Medicine 71(12):2150-2161, 2010.

[12] Muenning, P., Goldsmith, J.A., El-Sayed A.M., Goldmann, E.S., Quan, R., Barracks S., Cheung J., Behavioral Health in New York City: The Burden, Cost, and Return on Investment. Unpublished Raw Data, 2015.

[13] Druss, B. G., Zhao, L., Von Esenwein, S., Morrato, E. H., &

Marcus, S. C. Understanding Excess Mortality in Persons with Mental Illness: 17-year Follow Up of a Nationally Representative US Survey. Medical Care 49(6), 599-60, 2011.

14 Mitchell AJ, Malone D, Doebbeling CC. Quality of Medical Care for People with and Without Comorbid Mental Illness and Substance Misuse: Systematic Review of Comparative Studies. Br J Psychiatry 194(6):491-9, 2009.

15 Marder SR, Essock SM, Miller AL, Buchanan RW, Casey DE, Davis JM, et al. Physical Health Monitoring of Patients with Schizophrenia. Am J Psychiatry 161(8):1334-49, 2004.

16 Sokal, J., Messias, E., Dickerson, F.B., Kreyenbuhl, J., Brown, C.H., Goldberg, R.W., & Dixon, L.B. Comorbidity of Medical Illnesses Among Adults with Serious Mental Illness Who Are Receiving Community Psychiatric Services. The Journal of Nervous and Mental Disease, 192(6), 421-427, 2004.

17 Hennekens, C.H., Hennekens, A.R., Hollar, D., & Casey, D.E. Schizophrenia and Increased Risks of Cardiovascular Disease. American Heart Journal 150(6), 1115-1121, 2005. 150(6), 1115-1121.

18 Clark, N.G. Consensus Development Conference on Antipsychotic Drugs and Obesity and Diabetes. Diabetes Care. 27(2), 596,. 2004.

19 Norman C, Goldmann E, Staley B, Duchen R. Serious Mental Illness Among New York City Adults. NYC Vital Signs Volume 14, No. 2; 1-4, 2015.

20 Gilsanz, P.Walter, S; Tchetgen, E.J.et al. Changes in Depressive Symptoms and Incidence of First Stroke Among Middle-Aged and Older US Adults ," J Am Heart Assoc. 4: e001923, 2015.

21 Muenning, P., Goldsmith, J.A., El-Sayed A.M., Goldmann, E.S.,

Quan, R., Barracks S., Cheung J., Behavioral Health in New York City: The Burden, Cost, and Return on Investment. Unpublished Raw Data, 2015. Sources and methods for health care costs available upon request, DOHMH

22 Mayor of London. London Mental Health: The Invisible Costs of Mental Health, 2014.

23 New York City Department of Health and Mental Hygiene Bureau of Mental Health Medicaid Analysis Based on Salient NYS Medicaid System, Including Payment Cycles Through 1963, Unpublished Raw Data, 2015.

24 Milliman, Inc Commercial Insurance and Medicare analysis. (2015). Unpublished raw data.

25 Chapman, D.P., Whitfield, C.L., Felitti V.J., Dube S.R., Edwards, V.J, Anda, R.F. Adverse Childhood Experiences and the Risk of Depressive Disorders in Adulthood. Journal of Affective Disorders. 82: 217–2252004, 2004.

26 Halfon, N. Wise, P.H. and Forrest, C.B. The Changing Nature Of Children's Health Development: New Challenges Require Major Policy Solutions Health Affairs 33, no.12:2116-2124 doi: 10.1377/hlthaff.2014.0944, 2014.

27 Shonkoff, J.P. Boyce, W.T. McEwen, B.S. et al, Neuroscience, Molecular Biology, and the Childhood Roots of Health Disparities: Building a New Framework for Health Promotion and Disease Prevention, JAMA 301(21): 2252-2259, 2009.

28 McLaughlin, K. A., Green, J. G., Gruber, M. J., Sampson, N. A., Zaslavsky, A. M., & Kessler, R. C. Childhood Adversities and First Onset of Psychiatric Disorders in a National Sample of Adolescents. Archives of General Psychiatry 69(11), 1151–1160. http://doi.org/10.1001/archgenpsychiatry.2011.2277,

2012.69(11),1151–
1160.http://doi.org/10.1001/archgenpsychiatry. 2011.2277

29   Sharkey, P. The Acute Effect of Local Homicides on Children's Cognitive Performance. Proceedings of the National Academy of Sciences of the United States of America 107(26), 11733–11738. doi:10.1073/pnas.1000690107, 2010.

30   Mersky, J. P., J. Topitzes, and A. J. Reynolds. Impacts of Adverse Childhood Experiences on Health, Mental Health, and Substance Use in Early Adulthood: A Cohort Study of an Urban, Minority Sample in the US. Child Abuse & Neglect 37.11: 917-925, 2013.

31 New York City Department of Health and Mental Hygiene Bureau of Early Intervention, Identifying and Referring Children with Developmental Delays to Early Intervention Services. City Health Information, 2008.

32   2011/12 National Survey of Children's Health. NSCH 2011/12. Data Query from the Child and Adolescent Health Measurement Initiative, Data Resource Center for Child and Adolescent Health website. www.childhealthdata.org

33 Paus, T., Keshavan, M., Giedd, J.N. Why Do Many Psychiatric Disorders Emerge During Adolescence? Nature Reviews Neuroscience 9, 947-57, 2008.

34   U.S. Department of Health and Human Services. The Surgeon General's Call to Action To Prevent and Reduce Underage Drinking. U.S. Department of Health and Human Services, Office of the Surgeon General, 2007.

35 New York City Youth Risk Behavior Survey, 2013. Data are weighted to the population of NYC public high school students.

36 Ibid.

37 Margolin, G., Vickerman, K.A., Oliver, P.H., Gordis, E.B. Violence Exposure in Multiple Interpersonal Domains: Cumulative and Differential Effects. Journal of Adolescent Health 47; 198-205, 2010.

38 Duke, N. N., Pettingell, S. L., McMorris, B. J., and Borowsky, I. W. Adolescent Violence Perpetration: Associations with Multiple Types of Adverse Childhood Experiences. Pediatrics 124 (4), e778-e786, 2010.

39 New York City Department of Health and Mental Hygiene, 2015. http://www.nyc.gov/ html/doh/downloads/pdf/mental/underage-drinking-factsheet.pdf

40 Centers for Disease Control. New York City High School Youth Risk Behavior Survey, 2013. https://nccd.cdc.gov/youthonline/App/Results.aspx?LID=NY C

41 Hinterland, K, Sanderson, M, Eisenhower, D. Bullying Among New York City Youth. Epi Data Brief(37), 2013. http://www.nyc.gov/html/doh/downloads/pdf/epi/ databrief37.pdf.

42 Ibid.

44 Kessler, R.C., Berglund, P., Demler, O., Jin, R., Merikangas, K.R., Walters, E.E. Lifetime Prevalence and Age-of-Onset Distributions of DSM-IV Disorders in the National Comorbidity Survey Replication. Arch Gen Psychiatry 62:593-602, 2005.

45 Manzo, L., Jones, H., Freudenberg, N., Kwan, A., Tsui, E., Gagnon, M. The Psychological Well-Being of CUNY Students: Results from a Survey of CUNY Undergraduate Students Healthy CUNY Initiative, City University of New York, 2011.

http://web.gc.cuny.edu/che/cunypsychwellbeing.pdf

46 Dave, S., Petersen, I., Sherr, L., Nazareth I. Incidence of Maternal and Paternal Depression in Primary Care: a Cohort Study Using a Primary Care Database. Arch Pediatr Adolesc Med 164(11):1038-44, 2010.

47 Beardslee, W.R., Versage, E.M., Gladstone, T.R. Children of Affectively Ill Parents: a Review of the Past 10 Years. J Am Acad Child Adolescent Psychiatry, 37:1134-1141, 1998.

48 New York City Department of Health and Mental Hygiene, Bureau of Maternal, Infant & Reproductive Health PRAMS, 2012. http://www.nyc.gov/html/doh/html/data/ms-prams.shtml#postpartum

49 Pooler, J., Perry, D.F, & Ghandour, R.M. Prevalence and Risk Factors for Postpartum Depressive Symptoms Among Women Enrolled in WIC. Maternal and Child Health Journal 17.10 1969-1980, 2013.

50 McDaniel M and Lowenstein C. Depression in Low Income Mothers of Young Children: Are They Getting the Treatment They Need. Urban Institute, 2013. http://www.urban.org/sites/default/files/alfresco/publication-pdfs/412804-Depression-in- Low-Income-Mothers-of-Young-Children-Are-They-Getting-the-Treatment-They- Need-.PDF

51 New York City Department of Health and Mental Hygiene, Bureau of Early Intervention, Identifying and Referring Children with Developmental Delays to Early Intervention Services. City Health Information, 2008..

52 New York City Department of Health and Mental Hygiene, Bureau of Maternal, Infant & Reproductive Health PRAMS, 2012. http://www.nyc.gov/html/doh/html/data/ms-prams.shtml#postpartum

[53] Siegenthaler, M. Munder, T., Egger, M. Effect of Preventive Interventions in Mentally Ill Parents on the Mental Health of the Offspring: Systematic Review and Meta-analysis. Journal of the American Academy of Child and Adolescent Psychiatry 51, 1. 2012. 51, 1.

[54] Dixon L, Lucksted A, Stewart B, et al: Outcomes of the Peer-Taught 12-week Family-to-Family Education Program for Severe Mental Illness. Acta Psychiatrica Scandinavica 109:207–215, 2004.

[55] Pickett-Schenk SA, Cook JA, Steigman P, et al: Psychological Well-Being and Relationship Outcomes in a Randomized Study of Family Led Education. Archives of General Psychiatry 63:1043–1050, 2006.

[56] Brister, T, Cavaleri, M.A., Olin, S., Shen, S., Burns, B.J., Hoagwood, K.E. An Evaluation of the NAMI Basics Program. Journal of Child and Family Studies 21:439-442, 2012.

[57] Kessler Foundation, National Organization on Disabilities and Harris Interactive: 2010 Gap Survey of Americans with Disabilities, 2010. www.2010disabilitysurveys.org/index.html

[58] Bond, G.R., Becker, D.R., Drake, R.E., Rapp, C.A., Meisler, N., Lehman, A.F., Bell, M.D., & Blyler, C.R., Implementing Supported Employment as an Evidence-based Practice, Psychiatric Services, 2001.

[59] Butterworth, J., Hall, A., Smith, F., Migliore, A., Winsor, J., Timmons, J., & Domin, D.State Data: The National Report on Employment Services and Outcomes. Boston, MA: Institute for Community Inclusion, University of Massachusetts Boston

[60] Smith, F.A., & Bhattarai, S.Persons Served in Community Mental Health Programs

and Employment. Institute for Community Inclusion, 2011.

61 Office of Disability Employment Policy, Bureau of Labor Statistics, U.S. Department of Labor, Current Population Survey, 2010. www.bls.gov/cps

62 New York City Department of Health and Mental Hygiene. Community Health Survey, Unpublished Data, 2008.

63 Centers for Disease Control. National Intimate Partner and Sexual Violence Survey,2010. http://www.cdc.gov/violenceprevention/pdf/nisvs_report20 10-a.pdf

64 Bruce, M.L., McAvay, G.J., Raue, P.J., Brown, E.L.,Meyers, B.S., Keohane, D.J., Jagoda, D.R., and Weber, C. Major Depression in Elderly Home Health Care Patients.. American Journal of Psychiatry 159: 1367-1374, 2002.

65 Zisook S, Shear, K. Grief and Bereavement: What Psychiatrists Need to Know: World Psychiatry, 8: 67-74, 2008.

66 National Center for Health Statistics. Health, United States, 2012: With Special Feature on Emergency Care. Hyattsville, MD., 2013.

67 Gfroerer, J., Penne, M., Pemberton, M., Folsom, R. Substance Abuse Treatment Need Among Older Adults in 2020: The Impact of the Aging Baby-Boom Cohort, Drug and Alcohol Dependence 69 (2): 127-135, 2003.

68 Yamaki K, Hsieh K, Heller T. Health Profile of Aging Family Caregivers Supporting Adults with Intellectual and Developmental Disabilities at Home. Intellect Dev Disabil 47(6):425-35, 2009.

69 Lifespan of Greater Rochester, Inc., Weill Cornell Medical Center of Cornell University, and New York City Department

for the Aging. Under the Radar: New York State Elder Abuse Prevalence Study Self-Reported Prevalence and Documented Case Surveys, 2011.

[70] New York City Department of Health and Mental Hygiene. Community Mental Health Survey Unpublished Raw Data, 2012.

[71] New York City Department of Health and Mental Hygiene. Child Health Survey, 2009.

[72] Coyle C, Stayton C, Ha J, Norman C, Sadler P, Driver C, Heller D, Paone D, Singh T, Olson C. Suicide and Self-inflicted Injuries in New York City. NYC Vital Signs 11(1):1–4, 2012.

[73] Williams DR, Gonzalez HM, Neighbors H, Nesse R, Abelson JM, Sweetman J, Jackson JS. Prevalence and Distribution of Major Depressive Disorder in African Americans, Caribbean Blacks, and Non-Hispanic Whites. Archives of General Psychiatry, 2007.

[74] Breslau J, Kendler KS, Su M, Gaxiola-Aguilar S, Kessler RC. Lifetime Risk and Persistence of Psychiatric Disorders Across Ethnic Groups in the United States. Psychol Med 35(3):317-27, 2005.

[75] Gara MA, Vega WA, Arndt S, Escamilla M, Fleck DE, Lawson WB, et al. Influence of Patient Race and Ethnicity on ClinicalAssessment in Patients with Affective Disorders. Arch Gen Psychiatry 69(6):593-600, 2012.

[76] Metzl, JM. Power Psychosis: How Schizophrenia Became a Black Disease (New York: Beacon Press), 2011.

[77] Stockdale, Susan E. et al. Racial and Ethnic Disparities in Detection and Treatment of

Depression and Anxiety Among Psychiatric and Primary Health Care Visits, 1995–2005. Medical Care 46.7 668–677, 2008.

78 Wassertheil-Smoller, S, et al. Depression, Anxiety, Antidepressant Use, and Cardiovascular Disease Among Hispanic Men and Women of Different National Backgrounds: Results from the Hispanic Community Health Study/Study of Latinos. Annals of Epidemiology 24.11822-830, 2014.

79 New York City Department of Health and Mental Hygiene. Community Health Survey Unpublished Data, combined 2009-2010, 2012.

80 U.S. Department of Health and Human Services. Mental Health: Culture, Race, and Ethnicity—A Supplement to Mental Health: A Report of the Surgeon General. Substance Abuse and Mental Health Services Administration, Center for Mental Health Services, 2001.

81 Ibid.

82 Hankerson SH, Fenton MC, Geier TJ, Keyes KM, Weissman MM, Hasin DS. Racial Differences in Symptoms, Comorbidity, and Treatment for Major Depressive Disorder Among Black and White Adults. J Natl Med Assoc Jul;103(7):576-84, 2011.

83 New York State Department of Health Statewide Planning and Research Cooperative System, 2013.

84 Definition of SMI: Adults with Serious Mental Illness (SMI) currently or at some time during the past year had a diagnosable mental, behavioral or emotional disorder (excluding developmental and substance use disorders) that resulted in functional impairment that substantially interfered with or limited functioning in one or more major life activities. More specifically, SMI prevalence were determined using an algorithm from the National Survey on Drug Use and Health

that included age, scores from the Kessler-6 (K6) scale (six items which assess emotional distress), and an abbreviated version of the World Health Organization Disability Assessment Schedule (WHODAS) (eight items which assess functional impairment).

85 New York City Department of Health and Mental Hygiene. Community Mental Health Survey Unpublished Raw Data, 2012.

86 New York City Department of Health and Mental Hygiene, Bureau of Mental Health Medicaid Analysis Based on Salient NYS Medicaid System, Including Payment Cycles through 1963 Unpublished Raw Data, 2015.

87 Milliman, Inc. Commercial Insurance and Medicare Analysis. (2015). Unpublished raw data.

88 Unutzer, J., Depressive Symptoms and the Cost of Health Services in HMO Patients Aged 65 Years and Older, JAMA 1997.277;20, 1997.

89 Katon WJ, Lin E, Russo J, Unutzer J Increased Medical Costs of a Population-based Sample of Depressed Elderly Patients. Arch Gen Psychiatry 60(9):897-903, 2003.

90 Mental Health Continuity of Care Report NYS Office of Mental Health, BHO Performance Metrics Portal, 2014. https://my.omh.ny.gov/webcenter/faces/bho/reports.

91 A number of evidence-based, home-based clinical care interventions (Multisystemic Therapy (MST), Functional Family Therapy (FFT)) that crucially address both child and their family, improve outcomes and reduce utilization of high-intensity services over time. While costly, these alternatives are eventually far less expensive than treating these complex

needs in a fragmented, ineffective ways. For example, in New York State these families represent 5% of families but carry 50% of Medicaid costs because they receive disconnected hospital, emergency room, or other care rather than those methods best matched to need their needs.

92 Young AS, Klap R, Sherbourne CD, Wells KB. The Quality of Care for Depressive and Anxiety Disorders in the United States. Arch Gen Psychiatry 58(1):55-61, 2001.

93 Kessler RC, Berglund P, Demler O, Jin R, Koretz D, Merikangas KR, Rush AJ,,Walters EE, Wang PS; National Comorbidity Survey Replication. The Epidemiology of Major Depressive Disorder: Results from the National Comorbidity Survey Replication (NCS-R). JAMA 289(23):3095-3105, 2003.

94 González HM, Vega WA, Williams DR, Tarraf W, West BT, Neighbors HW. Depression Care in the United States: Too Little for Too Few. Arch Gen Psychiatry. 2010;67(1):37- 46. doi:10.1001/archgenpsychiatry 168, 2009.

95 Crystal, S., Olfson, M., Huang, C., Pincus, H., Gerhard, T. Broadened Use Of Atypical Antipsychotics: Safety, Effectiveness, And Policy Challenges. Health Affairs28, no., 2009.

96 Olfson M, Druss BG, Marcus SC. Trends in Mental Health Care among Children and Adolescents. New England Journal of Medicine 372(21):2029-2038, 2015.

97 OECD Guidelines on Measuring Subjective Well-being, OECD Publishing, DOI: http://dx.doi.org/10.1787/9789264191655-en , 2013.

98 Ibid.

55087891R00102

Made in the USA
Columbia, SC
10 April 2019